'We're always talking about social j ...ay
anything different about how we ... lly,
Genelle is carving out a space for ...
Ayishat Akanbi, writer

'*Communicate for Change* offers powerful ideas and methods for moving
beyond justice stalemates, clicktivism and Twitter arguments. Genelle's
intelligence, warmth and emotional literacy guide the reader through
the complex terrain of justice work, and will be valuable both for experienced activists and those new to agitating for change. I can already think
of many people I'll be recommending this book to - I'm excited to see
how it will enable change.'
Natalie Collins, activist and campaigner

'I love Genelle's work; she is skilful, impactful and curious. She communicates in a way I wish more people would: with nuance, confidence,
passion, and through a smart critical lens. I always learn a lot from her,
and readers will get so much from this book.'
Emma Gannon, author and podcaster

'Genelle Aldred is an advocate for independent thought and I always like
to read what she has to say. She has an understanding of how humans
actually work, rather than how we want them to. An important voice.'
Matt Haig, author

'Full of nuance, facts and 'aha' moments, this book is a huge step
forwards and away from the common circular arguments around structural inequality. [It's] the kind of huge step we need to take, should we
ever wish to make deep sustainable change in the world.'
Dr Sophie Mort, clinical psychologist and author

Genelle Aldred is a communications professional who holds an MA in Broadcast Journalism. She has worked as a broadcaster and newsreader for the BBC, ITV and ITN. Her experience also includes overseeing a digital strategy team for an international NGO and being a channel manager for a television station. Since leaving her career in journalism, Genelle has worked as a consultant for brands and individuals. She believes in the power of good communication for finding effective solutions.

Genelle has placed social-justice issues, media and politics at the heart of all that she does. She is often asked to speak at events and comment in the media. As well as being an ambassador for the Stillbirth and Neonatal Death Society (Sands), Genelle also sits on the committee for Women in Journalism and is a charity trustee.

Dedicated to

Krystal, Arooj, Luke and Ellis

I hope that we create a more just world for you to inherit

COMMUNICATE FOR CHANGE

Creating justice in a world of bias

Genelle Aldred

First published in Great Britain in 2021

Society for Promoting Christian Knowledge
36 Causton Street
London SW1P 4ST
www.spck.org.uk

British Library Cataloguing-in-Publication Data
A catalogue record for this book is available from the British Library

ISBN 978–0–281–08557–6
eBook ISBN 978–0–281–08558–3

Typeset by Fakenham Prepress Solutions, Fakenham, Norfolk NR21 8NL
First printed in Great Britain by Ashford Colour Press
Subsequently digitally reprinted in Great Britain

eBook by Fakenham Prepress Solutions, Fakenham, Norfolk NR21 8NL

Produced on paper from sustainable sources

Contents

Preface

People fail to get along because they fear each other; they fear each other because they don't know each other; they don't know each other because they have not communicated with each other.[1]

We haven't inherited a just world, so we have to create one. And it's not as if people haven't been trying to do exactly that. So what continues to get in the way?

I was a journalist for more than a decade. When I left journalism, I went to work in the field of international development. After a couple of detours, I ended up working in communications. My whole career has been about telling stories in some way, shape or form. The success of a story is often judged by how many people it engages, whether they understand it and, as a result, care enough about what they've heard to take the desired action. The realm of stories that touch people has led me to consider whether the aspect missing from the pursuit of a more just world is better communication.

On the one hand, I see how this idea might seem to downplay heinous activity; yet we know that most serious injustice begins on the fringes and migrates to the centre of society, which somehow allows it to take root. Most people at the centre can be swayed and persuaded to do what's right. However, we don't engage much there, which is not helped by the way the world currently communicates. In this case, I'd like to look at the other hand and to think about how we can know and understand one another better. What would that change?

Misunderstanding is everywhere. The COVID lockdown of 2020–1 resulted in more disconnection than ever between dissimilar people, because their paths no longer crossed as they did in the bustling, busy pre-COVID world. The killing of George Floyd and the repercussions of his death here in the UK brought to the surface racial tensions that have long been simmering. We couldn't turn away from them because much of the world was closed and there were no distractions. It's hard to say when it all came to a head because there were numerous flashpoints as different topics came up: our politics and politicians, the inequalities in health care, Black Lives Matter marches and government reports. Even the Royal Family didn't remain untouched by issues of race as news reports of a rift over questionable behaviour and words spoken circled the world. We just couldn't get away from the opposite sides of stories that were discussed, with no solution in sight. So, as things remain, there has been some progress towards the goal of a fairer and more equal world, but not nearly enough.

I am as apprehensive as I am passionate about adding my voice to the fray. I'm not a data or behavioural scientist; I'm not an academic: I'm writing this book as a frustrated onlooker who hopes for a world that will allow us all to fulfil our potential. I would love to see an end to circular and unfruitful conversations. One person can be limited in what he or she knows and can speak about. For me, as a Black woman, the need for a more just world is very personal. It's not about one particular incident; it's about the many incidents, conversations and struggles which have shown me that things have to be different and better.

My faith has also informed this view. As a result, my thinking leans towards service and justice. The faith I hold is a reminder that life is not just about *me*; it's always about *us* and those who will follow. We are responsible for either playing a part in building a fairer world or maintaining harmful structures of power that support the status quo. You may not have a faith or believe in God, particularly if you think that the Bible has often been used to support injustice, which, of course, is a misuse. The Bible actually teaches us that loving our neighbour as ourselves is one of the two greatest commandments (the other is loving God).

One of my favourite biblical illustrations of justice is the one in which Jesus saves the adulterous woman from being stoned (see John 8.1–11). He says that if anyone is without sin, he (or she) may cast the first stone. Jesus doesn't tell people that they must do this or that. Rather, he asks them to look inside. As a result, the people who were about to kill the adulterous woman all dropped their stones and walked away, and her life was spared. As we try to tell others what to do, how much honesty is missing from our communication about our own part in maintaining an unjust world?

As I mentioned above, I'm a communications expert and I want to focus on the aspects of communication and injustice. I am a Black, middle-class, heterosexual, able-bodied woman, and many of the examples I use are viewed through this lens. I could try to write about other areas to please those who might say, 'But you didn't mention this or that injustice.' But there still remain justice journeys for me to go on too. As you read, I hope that what you'll notice are those concepts and ways of thinking and communicating that apply to you and the social-justice issues you know intimately and care about deeply.

If there were a simple way of solving injustice, we would have done it. It's time to consider more complex and nuanced conversations. We can't do so, however, until we understand how we affect others by the way we live our lives and until we care enough to make adjustments. I look at communication from a strategic, some might say dispassionate, point of view. I hope to be pragmatic, direct and caring. I explore how we can all be solution-orientated thinkers, as I try to be, and, more importantly, solution-orientated communicators.

Acknowledgements

They say it takes a village to raise a child, and it takes the same to bring observations and words to life. There are so many people I am thankful for – for their support, words of encouragement, reading chapters and discussing my ideas. Thank you to Stephanie, Sebrina, Corrine, Sara, Ronke and Ayishat, to name a few. There was a tough moment when I wasn't sure if I could do this, and I messaged Emma and she told me to fight for my book. That advice sustained me, thank you. Thank you Sophie, my wonderful EA, who keeps me as organized as I can be (not very).

You don't become an opinionated observer of life who refuses to blindly follow by accident. My family are an ever-present and powerful source of inspiration. My parents, Bishop Dr Joe and Novelette Aldred, have led that charge. For the many blessings and clashes along the way, I am thankful. To my beautiful sisters, Marsha and Alethea, and my wonderful nieces and nephews, Krystal, Arooj, Luke and Ellis, I want to say thank you for always holding space for me.

To my wider extended family, from Grandma Pearline, who will cut you quick and help you see the truths that only elders see, to my Aunty Winsome, Aunty Gloria, Uncle Mikey, Aunty Julie and Aunty Marva (naming names only ever gets you in trouble!), and several of my cousins who are always boosting me up – Angela, Vicky and Anita (sorry I missed your wedding!) – I love you and all my extended family with a big love!

Too many other family and friends to name have prayed, encouraged, put up with my general absenteeism while I've worked and were still there when I needed a pick me up. Thank you Julia, Liz, Adriana, Zoe, Kiera, Tricia, Vanessa, Natalie. If I haven't included your name here, that's my head, not my heart. So many people have been part of this journey.

My dad said to me that writing a book is 'vulnerable and risky'. While the vulnerability is mine, the risk was the publisher's! Thank you to SPCK for taking a chance on me and this book. To Sam Richardson, I owe a debt of gratitude. Thank you for making this book better and assuring me that I didn't need to join the circus, as it would all be fine. Thank you, Alexandra McDonald, for your support during our chat on a London Tube train about a vague idea and since to now. Louise Clairmonte and Michelle Clark, you both helped my words to be better and clearer. To Joanne Pountney, Sarah Head, Sam Snedden, Rowan Miller, Rehema Njambi and Rhoda Hardie, a heartfelt thank you. Mark Read, thank you for working with me and my many opinions to get the cover just right.

I am grateful and blessed and thank God, from whom all blessings flow. The gifts of life and purpose never cease to astound me and help me to make sense of how to use my time well.

Thank you for picking up this book, telling someone about this book, promoting this book and helping it to have a part in us all, as we move forward to better conversations and a more just world.

1

Communicate for solutions

Winning hearts and minds

We have arguments rather than conversations around social-justice issues and the belief that we should all have access to equal economic, social and political opportunities. Arguments are, at best, ineffective at convincing others to open their minds or, at worst, antagonistic. For long-lasting change to occur, we have to win minds and hearts because, as Dale Carnegie says, we never win an argument, even when we're right.[1] The idea that we can shout people into goodness is not without merit and evidence; it can sometimes work, as the suffragette movement showed. When it does, the change is big but it is a rare phenomenon. Most loud efforts seldom provide enduring change that can be felt by many. They fade into obscurity, much to the anger of those who are desperate for change. I understand why people cause a commotion. The emotions and anger against injustice overflow – and rightly so – but do they make the people who need to change listen? Do loudness and anger achieve the goal? Are we measuring whether we made people pay attention – that they looked at and heard what we were saying – rather than whether the listening resulted in altered behaviours? Did we win hearts and minds or just the moral argument? If we failed to win hearts and minds, we will probably have to have the conversation again.

I can be a little bit impatient with a circular conversation, and my impatience can become apparent to the other person. When I see that the discussion keeps going round and round, I start to think it's a waste of precious time. It's not so much that I don't agree with or see what the person is saying; it's that I don't believe the argument is going anywhere. I like to know that we are going to try to solve the issue or just agree to disagree, draw a line under it and move on. This attitude can be challenging to others because I appear to have gone from invested

1

and engaged in a conversation to uninterested and eager to talk about something else. It might seem like a rejection to someone, when he or she hasn't finished making a point, even though that's not my intention.

We've all had those interactions in which we keep arguing, with no resolution in sight. Yet it seems that there are people who have a massive appetite for circular conversations, which often occur in social-justice spaces. We have been debating poverty, racism, sexism and the like for many years, with no apparent way of bringing them to an end or reaching a place in which most people believe that there is equality. We have argued, protested and made some progress with some individuals. Yet we have still ended up losing the argument with many of those we want to persuade to change because they see only the circular nature of the debate. They have not been convinced that there is a solution which involves them. Not only have some become uninterested in drawing a line and moving on but also others have doubled-down on their thinking in the process. Central to this problem is the fact that one side usually talks about how all this makes them feel while the other wants to understand what is required of them. This is why winning hearts and minds together must be the goal of communication around social-justice issues.

We can win just the hearts and see people engage on an emotional level, offering sympathy, empathy and shared frustration. But if we were to fail to win the minds, there would not be much rational thinking about how to improve things. If we were to win only the 'how' of the minds, but achieve no personal engagement, the result would be a series of edicts and proposals. Such ideas would quickly be dropped when the goals weren't met because there would be little emotional connection to power the momentum. Many don't aim to capture hearts and minds at all; instead, they engage at a surface level ('The person said such-and-such') rather than digging deeper to try to understand what's behind the words. Coupled with the default position of assuming that those with whom we disagree have bad intentions, the cross-purposes and crossed lines of communication position us for interactions that are unlikely to produce understanding.

My job as a communication strategist is not only to hear what clients say but also to perceive the communication behind what they say. My clients tell me what they would like to achieve and I have to listen

carefully to deliver what they truly want. For the clients to ge
they want, they, in turn, have to listen carefully to their audiences and
customers to give them what they want. Having a bottom line makes
such an exercise worth doing for businesses.

In the arena of civics, this listening system isn't often one into which
we pour the same amount of time or energy, probably because the
advantage in spaces outside business isn't quite so clear. For example, I've
witnessed people talking about and engaging in efforts such as 'radical
listening'. Usually, radical listening is applauded because someone sits
and says nothing, but when the end result isn't tangible change, we must
all question what is actually going on. Being heard may make the person
talking feel good for the moment – it will help him or her to feel seen,
which pleases both parties – but when that is the pinnacle of the interaction, how does that really affect the world we share? Engaging in this
way does not result in real, enduring change. Yes, both parties feel good
because, on one level, there has been a dialogue (of sorts), but when
concrete, radical action isn't taken, there will just be an endless cycle of
the same fruitless activities.

Some people have no stake in seeing a result because they are not
affected by the problem: 'What's in it for me?' is a highly motivating
factor for those people, and one that we would do well to recognize and
reward. The hope or fear of certain consequences is a significant modifier
of human behaviour. The impetus to make changes is simply not there
when people feel unconnected to certain issues.

I remember travelling on the London Underground with a friend
who is left-handed. She remarked how annoying it was, when she went
through the ticket barrier, that she had to stretch her hand across her
body to touch her ticket to the pad. The world is built for right-handed
people such as me; so the problem with the Underground ticket barrier
is one that I had never even thought about. It hadn't occurred to me
how, in big and small ways, the positioning of the touch-pad saves right-
handed people time and effort all day long. Have I written to Transport
for London to ask it to change the barriers to provide equal access for
left-handed and right-handed people? Have I done anything about it at
all? No. Am I a bad person for not caring enough? I thought about what
my friend said; I acknowledged the inconvenience she suffered, but I

didn't dwell on it. I moved on. This was an example of a seemingly minor problem that had no impact on me at all. This is why things don't change: when we aren't affected by a problem, we have no investment in solving it.

Whether the injustice is big or small, until people are invested, they will feel badly about it – and for you – but continue with life as usual. While it is a privilege not to have to face certain injustices, the belief that people *have* to do better is a myth. We all have to abide by the law, but no one has to be good and kind. We might want people to behave a certain way, but we have to remember that what we and others think goodness and kindness look like are not always the same. While we can apply a moral argument to the need for everyone to be good, fair and kind, I believe that we have to engage with people where they are, rather than where we would like them to be. Individuals can't know what they don't know, and they won't try to do better at something that doesn't concern them. That may be an unpopular view but, for me, starting from any other place results in no change and more frustration.

'A riot is the language of the unheard,' as Martin Luther King, Jr said.[2] Anger and emotion are there precisely because the injustices many of us face have been part of our lives for so long. We communicate as though the situation will never change, so we don't know how to talk to solutions. This despair also affects how we approach the issue. How do we begin to behave as though there were another way to win hearts and minds, if, indeed, they can be won at all?

Talking to solutions

I came to learn about talking to solutions by sitting outside my father's study, book in hand, listening to his phone calls, and hearing him deal with problems and manoeuvre people towards outcomes. I was around eight years old. I was fascinated by what he did. I didn't really know why I was fascinated or what was really happening, but it seemed interesting to a curious child like me who loved to learn.

At that time, Dad was a pastor at a Black majority church in Sheffield. He was also overseeing around eight other churches in that part of Yorkshire for the Church of God of Prophecy, which has its general headquarters in Tennessee and its UK national office in Birmingham.

Dad dealt with molehills and mountains, and with congregants and leaders. Churches are political places; what people say they want and the things they do are often convoluted because they wish to resemble Jesus while having all the human desires to be top dog, and engaging in the manoeuvring that entails.

Years later, I'm still curious about what makes people tick. I'm a talkative person, so others often assume that I'm not listening to them. I'm always listening, taking note of the subtext, reading between the lines, decoding what people are saying and trying to get to grips with what they mean, and, most importantly, where they're coming from. I can then make a plan about how I want to approach something – I'm a strategist to the core. Added to that is my tendency, from years of working in journalism, to ask questions and produce narratives[3] from the answers. I try not to lose sight of what I hope to achieve and which message I plan to distil to reach the desired – or required – outcome. There is a lot of mind (rather than heart) involved in what I do because big emotions can sometimes hinder communication, especially when they are not controlled. Nevertheless, as I've mentioned, despite my own preferences, there is a need for engaging both hearts and minds to bring about enduring change.

Social justice and issues of oppression naturally have big emotions attached, especially for those who are wronged. But for those who have not had similar experiences, the response to the same questions might be low-key or even unemotional. How do we get past that difference to allow a solution orientated conversation to happen?

Eager to Love by the Franciscan monk Richard Rohr is an inspiring book in many ways. In it, Rohr identifies something that many of us feel or sense is missing: a third way he calls 'Third Force' activity: 'When you honour both power and powerlessness, you quite simply come up with a third something, a very different kind of power.'[4] There is something that is missing from the conversation about injustice. The third way in this case could be nuanced disagreement, a way of being gracious towards the human being we are dealing with while not condoning his or her behaviour. The third-way approach might not be appropriate in every case. If, however, we were to hold that tension within us when we enter into dialogue, we would be more likely to affect others in both an emotional and a rational way, helping them and the conversation to move on from a place of hostility and antagonism to one of action.

Supremacy or superiority?

The two sides in these arenas of communication are perpetrators and victims, goodies and baddies, and problematic people and everyone else. I have yet to meet a person who isn't a problem – that is, if we understand 'being problematic' to mean holding views that someone else would find deeply offensive. While someone may call another individual out for his or her offensive views over ethnicity, the person doing the calling-out probably has some views that someone else would find offensive – around gender or sexuality, for example. So where does all this finger-pointing actually end?

We are not and cannot be the thought police. We all have biases, which take time to root out. We all have problematic views and the ability to offend others, no matter how inoffensive we might think we are.

The current thinking often dictates that a person *is* offensive when he or she offends someone. Yet the whole area of offence can never be just a one-way street, in which only one type of person offends and another type is offended. Offence can travel in both directions. It is a nonsense to say that we can be offended by 'offensive' people whom we think are problematic, but they cannot be offended by us because our views are 'right' and we aren't the problem. We can never alter anyone's thinking using this logic.

I'd like to remove the moral argument and consider a behavioural one. Offensive ideas and behaviours exist in us as much as they exist in others. Of course, we naturally see others as the problem and ourselves as the fixers, which prevents us from tackling the actual problem. We might think that we are good people, doing the work of justice and equality; we might think that we are reasonable and fair-minded, but I must burst that bubble by saying that we are offensive and problematic to someone, somewhere.

I have offensive and problematic thoughts too. Why? Because I am human. We all are, and we inevitably have blind spots about some areas of justice or the ways in which we view others who disagree with us, or

because of those we exclude from our visions of equality. We ?
acknowledge that we can be seen by others as problematic an
doing so will allow us to have better conversations that will r
change we want to see – conversations rooted in humility rather than in
an arrogance born from a sense of our rightness because we do the work
of the righteous. Arrogance resulting from attitudes of righteousness and
superiority is a barrier to having conversations that lead to change. We
should start with ourselves, but that is a tough place to start.

Many of the social-justice problems we face are grounded in feelings
of superiority and pride. Not many people want to see those characteristics in themselves, so they don't look for them or acknowledge them. As
someone wise once said, we all know that racism exists, yet no one seems
to know anyone who's racist. White supremacists are an exception; it is
often very clear who they are and what they believe.

Recently, I've been wondering why many liberals are so comfortable
with the term 'White supremacy'. I hadn't thought about it too much
until I had a conversation with the writer and artist Ayishat Akanbi. She
said:

> I refrain from using the term 'White supremacy' for a couple of
> reasons. One is that I believe that anyone who fears another race
> is suffering from an inferiority complex. The second reason is that
> I do not wish to inflate the egos of people who have mistaken this
> inferiority for superiority.

Her comment pushed me to consider what I thought the term meant
and to try to express what I believe to be the real issue that we have to
address.

White supremacy is a chimera: it's not a physical reality. It's an ideology
and, by frequently referencing it, we give it a life of its own and make it
seem more real than it is. Yet liberals of all ethnicities, especially White
liberals, embrace White supremacy as a concept because they don't
see themselves or the White people they like as subscribing to it. They
behave as if it were solely the terrain of the far right – the extremists –
and nothing to do with the decent people further to the left, because
liberals love everyone and White liberals are allies in every injustice.

After some exploration, I have come to understand the issue to be a 'superiority complex', which resides in many more people, but is often found in White liberals. When we examine language and actions carefully, we get to the root of why there is plenty of talk but no solution. The White superiority complex is the structure that props up racial injustice. How else could racial injustice reside in so many spaces, places and institutions? For those unjust systems to continue to affect our daily lives, they have to have reached a critical mass as society at large unquestioningly accepts unjust behaviour, and I would say that they have. Many of the people who would be classed as White supremacists hold little power (although they have some), but nothing, even the language, of that extreme ideology is welcome in most spaces.

If you were to bring me a person who says, 'I'm a White supremacist', I would know who I was dealing with. But if you were to bring me someone who thinks he or she understands equality, and has deeply held and unquestioned views of his or her own superiority, I would have no idea of who I was dealing with. It will take a while to see how deep those views are, as conversations and actions unfold over time. The clues often show up in language which reveals that the person sees himself or herself as a blend of activist and saviour.

Activist-saviours will often say things such as 'I wish people didn't need me to do X' while refusing to believe that anything can be done without them. They insist on showing others 'the ropes' of how to get stuff done rather than providing solutions, involving finding new systems and channels. They don't truly accept as their equals the people they claim to be 'helping'; they find it hard to believe that there are people of colour who do not need their help. They proclaim that they are always trying to 'support' others and want everyone to be aware that they are supportive. They crave to hear and know that others think they are good. Some activist-saviours defend some of the racist systems and structures, explaining why they're not so bad and that 'the world is just the way it is'. Because such activist-saviour thinking remains generally unaddressed, many of us know people who have this sort of superiority complex, although these individuals would not identify themselves as prejudiced.

If we were to uncouple intent from impact, I would say that, for many activist-saviours, there is no ill intent, other than wanting to be needed, which can make their behaviour more insidious. They genuinely believe that they are thinking and acting from a neutral or positive position but, when we look at the impact of what they do, we can see that they are far from helping to make the world a more equal and just place. Rather, the primary result is that their work lifts them up and they hold themselves above not only right-wing racists but also all the people they purportedly help. They hold up their liberal Whiteness as a beacon for all to see and acknowledge. We have to listen and observe closely because their outward language may not obviously reveal this; their behaviour, however, can fill in the blanks.

When activist-saviours are off the clock and socializing, are the kinds of people they 'help' represented in their friendship circles or other meaningful relationships? Do they invest time in such individuals and trust them with their secrets? Do they seek advice from those they 'help' on matters other than social-justice issues? Whom do activist-saviours hire to work for them? Whom do they recommend for work outside the arenas of diversity and inclusion?

When we look past the words to the actions, we can see whether someone considers us to be equals or projects to be worked on. To know that someone thinks of us as projects is never pleasant; it is insulting. However, not all people of colour are insulted: they either don't recognize what's going on or they do and play the game. For those who play the game, the prize is acceptance; they are accepted only when they allow themselves to be helped and, for some, that is all they seek. It is not a relationship of equals; so, personally, it's not a game in which I indulge. It is right to recognize when we need help or access, or when we can provide it. However, no one person can provide all the help that the world needs. Someone who possesses a superiority complex, though, will think that he or she can.

I was brought up in a home that didn't consider Whiteness the ideal; it didn't consider others as the ideal: there were no Joneses with whom to keep up. I was taught to do my best. That is why I have tended to give allyship[5] a wide berth. If the terms of allyship mean that I must be inferior, holding out a begging bowl for eternal kindness, I have to reject it because I'm a capable person with my own access and privilege.

Here, I should highlight that we call all instances of racial injustice 'racism' when some of it is due to ignorance or prejudice. Others, however, are examples of systemic racism. By gathering different types of injustice under the same umbrella, we lose the ability to take a nuanced approach to a specific situation. It is hard to be clear when all injustice is termed 'racism' and every case is pooled under that term. Treating someone who is merely ignorant as though they were racist doesn't further the conversation. Many people who have a superiority complex like and enjoy the company of people of colour. They don't intentionally seek to harm but their deeply held prejudice – as opposed to racism[6] – has a huge impact. Of course, prejudice isn't acceptable; it just needs a different conversation. However, when people have been made aware of their prejudiced ways of thinking but double-down and don't change, then I think racism is a fair call.

Prejudice and racism rooted in a superiority complex mean that Whiteness becomes synonymous with professionalism, the mainstream and the right way to do and to be. It's systemic in workplaces, in schools, in churches and other spaces. It's the reason why senior leadership positions in all spheres are often mostly filled by White people, specifically White men. Many White people do feel superior to Black people. I've seen it. I've felt it. I've experienced it, mainly from those trying to be progressive. I could fill a book with the many comments I've received that betray this attitude, from surprise at how well-spoken I am, through being told at work that I'm not well-read enough about a political issue (even though I do the reading!), to the lack of acceptance of my leadership and direction by junior, inexperienced people. Those who feel innately superior might not be racist but they don't think that Black people are capable; they don't think well of us in general.

This issue is a massive one because when we always see ourselves as superior, it's very hard to agitate for true equality. It's difficult to do so if we always think that those whom we're helping will never be ready to go it alone. It's an unexpressed position that is often adopted by all of us as we distance ourselves from our own unvocalized, prejudiced behaviours. These are the toughest behaviours to tackle and correct because of this silence, which is why systemic oppression remains.

This superiority complex is not just confined to White people. In the Western world, White people are the majority and hold much of the power. While their superiority complex holds people of colour back because we are easily othered,[7] it doesn't hold everyone back. There are lots of elements in the mix: injustice is not just about ethnicity; it's also about class and gender. We often use words such as 'privilege' to pertain to Whiteness, but privilege is not just about race or White people. The supersizing of White privilege[8] in a vacuum as the only and overriding factor in fairness negates many other factors, too, such as upbringing, access to services and education. It is disempowering for all people of colour because the subtext is that White privilege is too large a problem to overcome. If it can't be overcome, what are we trying to achieve with all our conversations?

When we consider privilege in a different country, where most people are Black or Brown, we have to wonder why there is an over-policing of groups who are poor and working class, when they have a similar skin colour to those doing the over-policing. We might say that such oppressive behaviours are learned from the colonial past, for example, and that's not wrong. But before the transatlantic slave trade existed, there were slaves and servants. This historical fact does not excuse such abhorrent behaviour; rather, it illustrates that there is something in human nature that likes to control, to dominate, to be on top and not at the bottom. However, the stark differences in skin colour – the clear otherness that divides the groups we term 'races' – makes it easier to differentiate 'them' from 'us'. The consequences are very far reaching, as we see today. It would be hard, nearly impossible in fact, to create an apartheid based on class that works all the time because some of the differences are not visible. An apartheid based on ethnicity is much easier, in which a few 'pass for White' but in which most are immediately identifiable.

As a Black woman, I have seen a kind of superiority complex in the Black community, where the familiar self-selecting, self-sifting behaviour goes on among people who all look similar to outsiders. The Black community has its own power structures and dynamics that identify who are the helpers and who needs help. None of us is ever far from this kind of divisive behaviour. We must come to understand how it hinders true change. We must all cultivate the ability to look deeply inside ourselves and acknowledge the bias and prejudice that we find. Then we can honestly highlight those areas in which we might be coming up short.

We all know how to treat other people well and with respect. And when we don't, we know. We know when we have chosen to converse with someone about a prickly issue, and when we have doubled-down on an attitude or shut down a conversation. In this regard, no one will ever be perfect, so an honest – rather than a faux-modest – assessment of ourselves will help to keep the conversation respectful and solution-orientated.

Space to disagree

We're not always good at disagreeing well. We're not always good at giving space to one another to share thoughts freely. We're not always good at respecting one another when the discourse gets tricky and someone says the wrong thing, even when it's not based in malice. If we genuinely want to find solutions, we have to be able to disagree in a better way. From a mental-health perspective, feeling and staying safe on both sides is also important. There are ways to be strong, direct and respectful. But, occasionally, it is necessary to leave the dialogue and it may be difficult to be kind about doing so. Nevertheless, when we can, we must try to engage well.

A starting point for solutions-orientated conversations is to consider the language we use and the different meanings people ascribe to words. Words have long being weaponized. For example, if the word 'woke'[9] means a way of being for me but is a slur for you and we begin to talk, we are not in the same book – never mind on the same page. My interpretation and your interpretation of the words we use can be radically different, which makes it hard when we suppose that we're talking about the same thing. Conversations about injustice are currently fractious partly because of this problem and because there's so much that hinders communicating well, such as polarized opinions, the political divide and so on. We become tied up in the unhelpful labelling of others, resulting in assumptions that cut both ways and prevent connection.

In an ideal world, when I say 'woke' and you hear 'woke', we under-stand it in the same way. There may be things that we do agree on. For instance, if we were to ask the questions 'Do you think we should have equality? Do you think that things could be better?', everyone would say, 'Yes!' Although we might be talking about different things, most people agree that this world is a place of inequality, and that it has to change. Yet, in more than 20, 30, 50, 100 or 400 years, all we have managed to do is make mostly cosmetic rather than deep, enduring changes. Surely, we have to consider a new approach. After all, doing the same thing over and over again and expecting different results is the definition of insanity. Although I'm certain that there is no silver bullet (and perhaps I'm naive in my thinking), surely the beginning of the answer to finding solutions is to rethink how we communicate and truly understand our attitudes and behaviours. We have to discuss those ways and actions rather than just who we think we should and could be.

Communication is one of the biggest tools for change we have and it can be used in a variety of ways. We each would do well to spend time considering our deeply held views and beliefs, especially the unvocalized ones, and to examine our own actions. We have to shake off the things that we are *expected* to think and to say. For instance, I can approach the conversation from the position of being a Black woman because it is the space I've inhabited all my life and from which I feel safest to comment. I know that not everyone will agree with my views, but that's all right because I cannot and am not speaking for all Black people everywhere. I can speak only for myself. I'm not speaking for women everywhere. I'm speaking only for myself. I'm not speaking for straight people everywhere. I'm speaking only for myself. I'm not speaking for people who have faith everywhere. We can disagree on how to make life better for all, but we must still speak, because I think one of the biggest issues we need to work on is our inability to have better conversations around issues of injustice.

We should not blithely say that we want to step into someone else's shoes; I think that's impossible. Rather, we should try to see someone else's situation as it is, from his or her point of view, and not as a problem to be resolved or dismissed from ours. It's easy for me to say, 'Well, you know, I've never been stopped by the police, so it can't be that bad.' But for a young Black man who has been stopped 38 times, the situation is quite different. He cannot look at me and expect me to understand fully the depth of what's going on because I've never had to deal with that degree of harassment. Even so, I can expand my thinking to encompass what he endures as part of the collective experience that I hold in my heart and mind. I understand that I've not experienced certain things, so my point of view is based on limited knowledge. If, instead, I were to play devil's advocate, I would be showing how little of his or others' experiences I understand. Playing devil's advocate would signal to others that I don't really believe them; so, personally, it's something I choose not to do.

We should be able to ask people outright whether they can explain more or say whether they disagree with us or don't believe our experiences. We must also be generous enough to acknowledge that some people will not believe what they haven't seen or experienced, and may choose to walk away from conversing about the issues. After all, our flourishing and healing cannot be solely dependent on being heard and accepted. I can be big enough to disagree with people strongly and extend the grace I would wish to receive. I don't want to downplay the differences; rather, I choose to engage with others as I would like them to engage with me. I don't want to demand that someone sees my humanity while I refuse to see theirs. In so many subtle ways, we can maintain the power dynamics by saying and believing that other people are so much more powerful or weaker than we are.

So we need to have a basic level of understanding but, before that, there has to be a basic level of respect for those who lack knowledge about others' experiences, even when we think they 'should' know more. It is tricky: every situation comes with its own caveats and no one can account for every single one of them. If, at the very least, we were open to trying to assess the situation in front of us, rather than seeing a stereotype, it would help us to reach individual and collective answers more quickly. As we communicate, we can bring solutions to the actual, current conversations – with all their nuances, complications and caveats – rather than to the conversations that we wish we were having.

2

Fake news

The news has never been neutral – almost anything that involves humans isn't – yet it has long been viewed as a trusted source of information. And if the news isn't neutral, then it cannot be completely accurate. Nevertheless, we have been using it as a guide of sorts to understand what is true. Our faith in the news can be harmful, especially when it comes to understanding people who are not like us and cultures that we don't know much about. This is part of the reason that we find ourselves where we do: the news we look to – to find accurate information about events and people – is not always trustworthy. It can lead to further misunderstanding because we want trust and believe it to be neutral, accurate, transparent and honest.

In the past few decades, there have been major changes to news distribution: there is now 24-hour rolling news, and current affairs are also readily available through the Internet, including via social media. The proliferation of outlets has caused our perception of the news to swing in the opposite direction – to mistrust. In the short decade and a half that I worked in news broadcasting, I saw that where it was once wholeheartedly trusted, it grew to be considered by many as a source of biased misinformation and propaganda that sometimes borders on the dangerous.

Has the news changed or have we? Perhaps the issue encompasses a bit of both.

Who benefits?

Most news comes from three places: first and second, the Press Association and Reuters (known as the 'press wires' or 'wires'), and, third, directly from other organizations, such as the police or the government. So the news that we see has one source or another, it's spun in several different ways, by the journalists and organizations writing the subtext, which they do. This process isn't entirely mysterious: ten of us might see the same incident between two people; we would all have different thoughts about who started it, how it started and why. Was one person being aggressive or defensive? And if we were to report on what we saw, several factors would affect our version of events, and those factors mainly reside in us. People are people and, whether they have training or not, journalists are just people.

But what about the data often used to back up news stories? As a big fan of data, I always say they don't lie – and they don't – but we can use data to tell various stories, as all data can be interpreted in a number of ways. For example, we hear a lot about absent Black fathers. In fact, from the news, you would think that half or more of Black families in the UK have absentee fathers. In reality, the UK 2011 census showed that single-parent families comprised 18.9 per cent of the Black population. So, while we could say that a Black family is twice as likely to have a single parent as a White family, the figures tell us that four in five Black families have two parents. It all depends on how you spin it. Data don't lie; they tell multiple stories. But on the news, which is the statistic we hear and how do we hear it? The most sensational – not the most salient – facts are usually chosen to keep us interested. After all, highlighting that one in five Black families has a single parent just isn't as arresting as saying that they are twice as likely to be fatherless.

Let's stay with the fatherless-family scenario. To add weight to a certain interpretation of the data, guests are invited on to the news, in some cases to confirm the 'fact' that too many Black families are without fathers, and some of those guests will be Black. If I have a criticism of certain guests on the news, it is that they tend to join in with this performance. They, too, will wring their hands and say how bad the situation is, often without having researched other figures for themselves. Guests of this sort often have a vested interest in the story; they can be from special interest organizations that are funded to solve particular problems. So whom does it really benefit to tell the story this way? The need to make storytelling compelling can get in the way of nuanced truth.

When I think about singular narratives[1] that I have developed, one that stands out concerns a visit I and some colleagues made to Malawi in south-eastern Africa. On landing in Malawi, I was very surprised to see how green it was, as was the camera crew with me. We had all expected a dry, hard and barren land because we were there to film a story about the lack of rain, but it wouldn't stop raining! Of course, we didn't film and broadcast the rain and verdancy because they didn't convey the story we wanted.

This anecdote about Malawi illustrates an important factor in why certain stories are emphasized over others. In development, for example, they must consider their bottom lines, so charities don't report the situations that have been resolved, in order to generate income; they prefer to tell their audiences about the problems. Informing people about what has been solved does not motivate them to respond in quite the same way; therefore, because making or raising money is the key reason for the stories, the focus is on what remains to be done. We still have to work out how to report solutions with the same emphasis that we report problems. Perhaps we haven't because to do so is too complicated and nuanced, and it wouldn't make money.

We often see this kind of agit-prop repeated in the news: problem-telling in preference to problem-solving. When someone benefits, to a greater or lesser degree, from the way in which the news is told, the chances are that someone else is not benefiting and, indeed, is possibly being harmed – again, to a greater or lesser degree. More balanced reporting would involve a greater attempt to reflect positive Black family stories and hopeful development pieces to counter the negative ones. In both cases, continually telling the story in a certain way leads to an accepted big picture. As a result, it doesn't take too much to encourage people to think in certain ways about what they see on the news. Whole theories can be constructed and passed on as truth, resulting in recipients of the news viewing a whole section or group of people through the filter of a singular narrative, despite the recipients' having little or no knowledge of their own to counter what they watch.

We ought to reflect on the news we consume in a considered way, but we often don't. We shouldn't be wary of the news because those broadcasting it are necessarily evil; they aren't. They're humans with reasons – conscious and unconscious – for spinning things a certain way. However, when we understand that this powerful tool may not always be used for the greater good, we will take the time to educate ourselves more fully before using it as a measure by which to judge society and others.

The interesting thing is that we all hold the power to communicate and have the ability to bring more truth to any situation. We are part of the glue that holds everything together. These systems and structures do not stand alone in a vacuum and they cannot stand without support. We can and should talk about all the ways that we could collectively contribute to change.

How long has it been fake?

The easiest way to shoot a media piece down now is to call it 'fake news'. When we label something untrue, then we don't have to engage with it. Increasingly, we see politicians use this tactic. Unfortunately, because they are in positions of leadership, their behaviour is seen and amplified.

Although the term 'fake news' became popular in 2016, it had been used before:

> [the] Merriam-Webster [website] points out, '*Fake news* appears to have begun seeing general use at the end of the 19th century.' The post cites several news articles from the 1890s, including an 1891 piece in *The Buffalo Commercial* (Buffalo, NY) that optimistically declared, 'The public taste . . . certainly has no genuine appetite for "fake news" and "special fiend" decoctions, such as were served up by a local syndicate a year or two ago.'[2]

It is important to bear in mind that news lacks neutrality (which in my opinion makes it 'fake') because of the esteem in which it has been held and how much it has shaped cultures, behaviour, and the acceptance and rejection or dismissal of issues. We could also call it 'false news' when it sensationalizes or lies about the facts presented. We should ask whether it matters when broadcasters and journalists present stories from a certain angle for public consumption. It certainly matters to those who are being misrepresented. For there to be change, it has to matter to us all. There is little point in our becoming angry; we should push for solutions.

Before social media became mainstream, and when many more jobs were 9-to-5 ones in workplaces, most people would come home and watch the news to find out what had happened since the morning, when they had read the papers. A couple of programmes were the main sources of information and there was little dispute about how events were presented. These days, the proliferation of channels and news organizations reporting their particular versions of events means that many people no longer believe everything they see on the news is 'the truth'. Consumers of news now differentiate between subjective and objective truth, and the media are often seen as purveyors of subjective truths. There is a sea of information from multiple sources, resulting in an overload when most of us just want the facts to be clear.

I don't believe the news was ever the guiding star that we thought it was. However, it was all we had, so we felt sure of it and what it represented. Now, we feel the loss of that certainty as it becomes increasingly difficult to know who is telling the truth. Although we have more access to stories outside our worlds, we have fewer ways of understanding what we see and fewer ways of knowing what is opinion, what is fact and what is in between. So, rather than broadening our horizons, all this choice seems to funnel us towards what is familiar and comfortable – towards the stories and stereotypes with which we have an affinity or that make sense to us. If we receive new facts that don't match what we think we know, we are likely to stick with the old tried-and-trusted information.

We could call these spaces of comfort, these 'echo chambers' – from which we choose to receive only news with which we agree – our 'safe chambers' because they reinforce our 'rightness', and confirm that we are the good and reasonable people we think we are. We seek the news outlets that will do that for us, rarely searching for the ones that dispute the version of events we prefer. To do so would be too confrontational and would potentially destroy the singular narrative that we like. The story we choose *is* our truth; it preserves our comfort.

Clickbait

In the arena of the news, it's more important than ever to be the first to break stories. It is imperative to help the reader to understand the message quickly, so the pieces have to be easily digestible. This competition for an audience results in what is termed clickbait: misleading headlines designed to make people click on an article. The more sensational the story headline, the greater the number of people who will choose to read that version of events. But – surprise, surprise – not much in the article correlates with the exciting headline. Nevertheless, people are reeled in; they click!

In the chase for an ever-increasing number of readers, I would say that many journalists have found themselves writing headlines that don't truly reflect their articles. I have done it. I've looked for the best angle to increase that audience share because larger numbers usually result in more advertising revenue or greater influence. When you're immersed in this activity, it doesn't seem to be as intentional or as sinister as it sounds. Whatever the intent, the cumulative effect of the pattern of repeated clickbaiting is one of the reasons social media have eroded trust in the news. Many people find it difficult to discern what is truth and what is spin.

When the phrase 'alternative facts' entered the picture a few years ago, things began to look extremely bleak for objective truth. The very definition of a fact means that there's no such thing as an alternative one. To the reading and viewing public, the term 'alternative facts' just seems to confirm their belief that news is fake and untruths abound. On the one hand, the sensationalizing and simplifying of stories and headlines has come to be an accepted part of the news landscape. On the other, the idea that it might simply be about increasing audience share doesn't mean that the impact is benign. The sensationalizing happens over and over again, focusing on particular groups of people. If those who receive the news through various media don't know the true stories, the simplified, sensationalized versions will fill the void of knowledge, and, over time, these versions will be assumed to be true.

Hillary Rodham Clinton, speaking in a documentary called *Hillary*, highlights how anything that is continually repeated becomes 'the truth':

'Here is what I want people to understand,' she says. 'Even when something is disproved, people remember the allegation was made . . . that kind of constant character assault takes a toll. Even people who are supporters [and] friends, they brush it off. They don't believe it. But it still has a little space in the back of their heads, so if something else happens, that space gets a little bigger. That's been the story of my public life.'[3]

Hillary calls herself the 'most investigated innocent person'. I cannot say whether or not she is guilty of the things reported about her, but she's right on this point, her comment about the 'little space in the back of' of her friends' heads. If that small gap, which contains a bit of the lie, exists in her friends' minds, how much bigger is the gap in the minds of strangers? Most of us know Hillary only through the media. What are your views of her?

We might think that we are unaffected by the negative stories but we're not – not entirely. It wasn't until one of my sisters had a Muslim friend who spent time with us, including at large family gatherings, that I looked more closely at stories that conflated terrorism with Islam. I began to choose to see Muslims differently: as a group of individuals who do not act in an homogeneous way.

Let's think about the portrayal of young Black men in the news. We usually see them in relation to stabbings, drugs and gangs. This representation criminalizes all Black men by association. If the news is our primary source of information about Black men, those stories of crime will, over time, become our 'truth' about them. The idea that Black men are dangerous is planted deep down in our psyche. These thoughts may not manifest themselves as a visceral reaction until we find ourselves in a situation with a young Black man or men. If we were to meet such people walking down the street (which isn't a crime), where would our minds go to first? Would we automatically think about safety and that we might have to fight or flee those whom we *perceive* as dangerous?

The problems arise when we try to deny that we ever have such thoughts. The thoughts themselves aren't necessarily the problem: it's what we do because of them that is. Do we lean towards or away from attitudes that are rooted only in incidents that we've seen and never experienced?

Even in my mind, this tide of information has left a residue. However, because I'm personally acquainted with a large number of Black men, who are the kinds of human beings many aspire to be, I know that I don't need to fear unless they are *actually doing* something of which I should be afraid.

When it comes to news and media in general, there are singular narratives about minority ethnic groups. Black people are not an homogeneous mass; we are as complex a group as any other. It is grossly inaccurate, therefore, to use the shorthand term 'Black and minority ethnic' (BAME) to amalgamate hugely disparate peoples, encompassing many cultures, classes and sexualities. Even so, the news and media continue to present stories about 'BAME people' doing X, Y or Z. Why the mass singular narrative? One of the most shared tweets I've written was this one:

> The extent to which language is weaponised is interesting. Last week, it was 'violence' and protesters 'antagonising' the police for #BLM. This week, there are 'scuffles'. This is why newsrooms need greater diversity to guard against inherent biases that come through language use.[4]

We judge White men by what we know of them. They have many roles: there are White male CEOs, experts, criminals and terrorists. The media don't define who they are for us because they continually show the variety and complexity of this group. As a result, we're more likely to take White men as we find them and not fear them.

We always have the opportunity to examine our reactions and to work out where they come from. We might have had a poor experience with an individual or individuals from a certain group, to which are attached valid thoughts or feelings. When we encounter other people from that group, is it fair to react to them based on the thoughts and feelings associated with the previous, poor experience? We should avoid responding in the same way to every person we deem to be part of a particular group. After all, the millions of young Black men in the world, for example, can't all be similar. I've had some unpleasant experiences with White female bosses. Does that make all White women employers unpleasant? I don't think so. I had a lovely one who is now a close friend; if I had used another, less likeable, White woman as a marker for her, I would have missed out on so much.

'Fake news' may be defined as a mechanism we use to remain immune from seeing the world in a certain way. No matter how hard we try not to be, we are products of what we consume. We are continually being confronted with what is in us. Rather than pretend otherwise or berate those whom we consider deplorable, we should examine our own behaviour and consider why we feel the way we do. Which emotions arise and what do we think as we consider the ideas that are presented? What is our actual experience of certain situations and people? The media should not dictate to us what and who those are.

If we took the time to think and break through the assumptions that neither serve us nor the world well, we would be much more circumspect in forming our opinions, and more willing and able to take people as we find them. Of course, human beings must be assessed on their individual merits; there are, undoubtedly, some whom it is best to avoid.

What I often find is that people from mainstream culture can be whoever they want: complex and multidimensional. Those who are othered are more likely to be stereotyped. I have consciously worked on building a circle of friends who are not like me culturally. Knowing them broadens my horizons and allows me to see the world through different lenses. I try to understand other cultures through the eyes of those who belong to them, not through any kind of media filter. I refuse to let the media's intent to make me click, or to keep watching a news story, have an impact on the way I do or don't understand others.

Neutrality

In the UK, news programmes aim to be unbiased. Achieving lack of bias is, however, literally an impossible task. News is not formed in a vacuum; with human involvement, inevitably, comes fallibility and bias. The only way to prevent this problem would be to have a media team so diverse that it would include most cultures, ways of thinking and points of view. Only then could a news outlet ensure that the coverage of an item would be as fair and evenly balanced as possible. This is seldom, if ever, the case. What we usually view or read is true but it's often presented out of context and includes only what the editor considers important. And the decision about what makes the news is based on two practical points: content availability and whether the newsroom is adequately staffed.

Different media have different impacts. On the radio, the news is told only with voices and, if you're fortunate, ambient sounds; they are all you need to tell a compelling story. On TV, however, to capture the audience's interest, you also have to illustrate the piece with images, preferably of people. If there are no pictures, then the item isn't suitable for TV (unless it is literally the most extraordinary and important story of all time). Great story; no picture – not news. So, when we've discarded the items we can't show, we have to decide whether we have the staff to cover the stories that are worth filming. Once these points have been considered, we can start to build the news agenda. Many important stories are omitted because of these practical concerns, which are highlighted by a couple of newsroom sayings: 'Man walks dog – not news. Dog walks man – news' and 'If it bleeds, it leads'.

Often, 'outliers' (the stories that are rare, extremely bad or exceptionally positive) are at the top of the news agenda. The outliers are usually reported more than the normal stories of life, and so, because of the power of the storytelling and their trust in the storytellers, the public tends to become more afraid of events that are unlikely to happen. For instance, an individual is very much more likely to die in a car crash than in a terrorist incident.[5] But the time the media spend dwelling on deaths caused by terrorism vastly outweighs the time they take to discuss casualties from road traffic accidents. This comparison illustrates why and how the media affect our perceptions and the ways we think. When terrorist incidents happen, the news is saturated with them: the deaths have a huge impact; the incidents frighten us because we begin to believe that they could happen at any time, anywhere. In reality, we should be far more afraid of motor vehicles. But we're not. It may be that, because we use our cars so often, we'd prefer not to engage with this statistic; safe-chamber thinking would suggest that. However, the point here is that selective presentation of the news causes millions of people to have a greater fear of rarer dangers than more common ones.

Briefly mentioned earlier was the role of the editor, which is an aspect of the lack of neutrality in the news. In the process of deciding the news agenda, ultimately, one editor is in charge of what the viewers at home see; one individual is running the whole operation, which means that the fallibility of a person's singular narrative comes into play. Inevitably, the editor brings his or her own biases into the decision-making, even when working closely with a team. We all think different things are bad or good; we have varying levels of tolerance for the evils that are in the world. While those who make the decisions are not necessarily bad people (although some of them might be), they have a view, which directly affects what we see. For example, if an editor doesn't believe that the climate is changing, is he or she likely to give more air time to the climate-change campaigner or the denier?

For a very long time, the people making the choices about the news agenda have belonged to a certain demographic, sex and ethnicity. They have set specific singular narratives that they carry within themselves. Their views, which are not the objective truth, are transmitted into millions of living rooms by those who are a familiar presence – newsreaders – whom we tend to believe. Almost as if by osmosis, the transfer of beliefs and ideals occurs: the way the editors see the world becomes the way we see the world; we watch the news and imbibe their non-neutral perspective. There is infinite power and influence in this process. Even when these individuals sincerely believe that the choices they make are right and essential for shaping the views of the nation, what they do can be manipulative – whether intentional or not.

All these systems and processes of storytelling and decision-making are handed down through generations. Of course, some things alter as technologies advance and attitudes change but the mechanics remain the same. An editor trains a successor and shows him or her the ropes; experienced journalists make those same ropes known to rookie journalists. Almost all systemic issues are rooted in process-driven habits.

For too long, we've failed to question deeply what we see and consume. We haven't asked who benefits from the system and how that relates to the way stories are told. Thankfully, some people are beginning to ask these questions now, but it doesn't mean that we have to entirely reject the news. Rather, we have to consider how the main sources of information affect our perceptions of people who are different from us. We should be open to seeing that we might have wrong beliefs stemming from an editor – a single individual – who has his or her own questionable opinions. Rather than just accepting what we watch and read, we can intentionally become open to finding out more about the world, to giving ourselves a more rounded view.

The news bias

The big media window through which we view the world might be slightly left-leaning or right-leaning, but the ideas that we gather about what's going on are crafted for us. When the media are our main source of information about others, we can only know as much about the world as the media know or are willing to explore. My personal view is that I'd rather wade through the biases and gain an understanding of what's going on than be completely uninformed. But for some, the lack of trust is so profound that they don't watch the news at all. The thought of 'wrong' ideas and ideals being spread by osmosis troubles them. I understand that view; unfortunately, no news outlet is perfect. Added to that, those who distrust the media are jaded at continually being shown the worst humanity has to offer. The news, in the main, seems to be so negative and grim to watch.

I have to say that, in recent years, there has definitely been a change in the news and its delivery. (I have many friends in the news and media, so I'll tread carefully.) Yes, it's always been presented from the basis of someone's world view and, yes, it's always been crafted. Even though I understood this, after being a newsreader for many years, I no longer thought that I was contributing to the world in a way that I liked. I no longer believed that what I did truly informed people. I thought that, rather than helping the public to become knowledgeable about current affairs in a well-rounded way, I was part of a machine that was making the world a more fearful place. Every day, I would say in effect, 'These are the worst things that have happened today – with pictures, just in case you don't get it.' It did not bring me joy. I became so desensitized to some of the awful things I saw that I was almost emotionless. For example, for me, after hearing the word 'refugee' over and over again, individuals who had hopes and dreams became a faceless, anonymous group. Repeatedly relaying stories about crime, too, meant that I stopped thinking about those who suffered: the victims.

The effects of 24-hour news and social media

There are many reasons why the news and our attitudes towards it have become what they are. Two things, in particular, have been instrumental in shattering our illusions and making us distrustful: 24-hour rolling news and social media that almost never shut down. These two have had a profound effect on the ways we see others: some very positive; others not so much. This influence on our beliefs occurs mainly because of the continually quick pace at which the news is delivered. Something is always breaking and urgent; it's a cycle that never ends.

I believe that the speed of the news cycle affects our opinions and beliefs, and there are several factors which converge, causing audiences to mistrust it.

In the beginning, there were only the BBC's news programmes, which were on at specific times. Now there are hundreds of news outlets, all jockeying to tell us the same story while also slanting certain elements to gratify their loyal audiences. When a camera is angled in a certain way, it can make a crowd look larger or smaller. One agency will choose politicians' comments that support a certain view; another will focus on different quotes to show an alternative side of the story. Then carefully chosen commentators and experts will expand on it all. These different elements offer us not only the chance to understand that there are many ways to see a story but also the opportunity to realize that the version we've chosen might not be accurate. We've discovered that one source won't or can't report everything. We also know that all the different news outlets, although reporting the same story, can reach very different conclusions. From this we can see that they can't all be telling the objective truth.

We can also follow the news in real time, rather than watch a product that's been edited and crafted. I remember that, when my family got cable (as it was known then), my first real encounter with rolling news was watching O. J. Simpson – a US actor, broadcaster and former sports star – speeding down a road in a white Ford Bronco on Sky News. The year was 1994 and, like millions of others, I was glued to the TV screen. I don't wish to debate the outcome of Simpson's murder case here, but,

I thought, why would an innocent man run? As we watched him being chased by the police in real time, a story was already beginning to play out. I didn't know then that I'd become a journalist, but I was fascinated. The power of those pictures held my attention. They showed me a world and a person I didn't know, and I became invested in the outcome. I would come home from school and watch O. J.'s trial, fascinated by evidence such as the bloody glove. I was 12 years old and I was gripped. Then . . . O. J. got off! That didn't quite fit the singular narrative that had been unfolding. The fallout continued for many years afterwards.

Rolling news and channels that are on all day and night have to be filled with content. As they have to be fed continually, the quality and variety of what goes in is at times questionable, simply because of the volume. (These days, I switch off the TV when I hear the same news at least four times in one hour.) As well as requiring a never-ending stream of material, TV and social media have become increasingly intertwined over time: TV tells us what's happening on social media and social media tell us what's happening on TV. For both, that's 168 hours a week that have to be filled. The social-media timeline is always moving; if you want to stay on top and be first – by getting the bait clicked, the views and the followers – you have to feed that insatiable timeline continually with as much news content as you can, preferably more than what your competitors are supplying. When all the agencies and outlets are doing the same thing, with similar aims and with the same news, how does yours stand out?

When I studied journalism, I was taught that there is a difference between what is in the public interest and what the public are interested in. This distinction is slight but important; in trying to keep people's attention on continual broadcasts, the emphasis on capturing and holding people's interest has resulted in much 'non-news' being delivered. Non-news can be salacious, bizarre, malign or benign. It's not what we would have called news in the past, when the pieces selected had, as a threshold, of being in the public interest and had to fit into a much shorter span of time. So, the media outlets' need to fill their schedules with non-news has left many of us bereft of confidence in the content. When there is genuine breaking news, it is usually reported obsessively and then forgotten in a few days. The media will deliver, in the main, whatever holds the audience's attention at a particular moment.

The Internet has greatly democratized the sharing of information. In the past, when you wanted to reach a great many people with your ideas and opinions, you had to go through the traditional media. Social media have changed all that by widening even further the democratization of broadcasting and publishing. Literally, anyone can tell everyone anything at any time. This revolution in the sphere of sharing content means that stories traditionally left out of a crafted world view can now be aired. Also, people who were once silenced and had no access now have platforms from which to promote their views without any filter.

On the positive side, this democratization has resulted in justice being done because citizens were on the spot to film criminal incidents as they were happening. News cameras would struggle to be at a scene just as an event was unfolding owing to little, if any, warning. As a result of the public sharing live information, the world has witnessed some heart-breaking events. But before people were able to film incidents on their smartphones, hearts were breaking and it was going largely unreported. This kind of citizen journalism alone has pushed many news outlets to review what to do now that the broadcasting space is no longer so tightly controlled.

On the negative side, with the flood of news and the advent of the citizen journalist also comes misinformation on a much wider scale. For some, this is a new kind of power, with little or no accountability or responsibility. A damaging untruth can travel far and wide very quickly. We can no longer pull back from the way social media work: there are celebrities, commentators, influencers and more, all in the mix, sharing their views. This situation will not end: Pandora's box has been opened; the genie is out of the bottle.

Politics have become particularly poisonous because of the flood of news, misinformation, untruths and deluges of views, which never stop. Through buying social-media adverts, nation-states can interfere in other countries' elections by influencing individuals' decision-making and choices. There is a critical mass here – narratives become self-sustaining and grow. Social media are free and accessible to all, so it is a massive space in which to market ideas and beliefs. To make things worse, the sense of anonymity that many users of social media have has lowered their inhibitions, so they can spew hatred at politicians and anyone with whom they disagree. For these reasons, we should be rather more discerning about what we see on these platforms, particularly because it has become so easy to pitch something as news that isn't actually news.

These examples only scratch the surface. I want to point to the combination of 24-hour news and social media, which influence people who no longer feel that they have a trusted source of information. Because we're subjected to an overwhelming avalanche of content, we choose to find solace in what we know; our world shrinks to include only what we believe to be true. How else can we even begin to sift through everything that's on offer, particularly now that one of the main ways we learn about the world is through an extremely distorted lens. It was always distorted but, with no other quick or visible avenue of becoming informed, it made sense.

But the question remains: how can we come to understand more about others?

How do you know what you know?

On average, throughout our lifetimes, each of us will know about 400 people very well.[6] Given that an individual can know only so many others, we have to rely on additional means of gaining knowledge to understand our world more fully. It's one thing to be acquainted with lots of types of people; it's another to know and understand them all. Engaging in relationships with others, especially those who are different from us, is powerful. It helps to break down social barriers. The more we know and learn about other human beings, the more the world opens up for us.

Until fairly recently, the 400 people we knew well would have been mostly those who lived near us: people who were like us, including family. Nevertheless, the curious have always sought to know more about the world beyond their own locale; they have tried to expand their world view and increase their knowledge through books and, now, the Internet.

Reading transports us to other worlds. Books can't reveal everything, but they open a window and can ignite an interest in something of which we knew little or nothing before. As an avid reader, I have learnt many useful, and some useless, facts from reading different kinds of literature. I remember enjoying the novel *Half of a Yellow Sun*,[7] through which I discovered a bit about the Biafran War and Nigerian Igbo culture; a Charles Dickens book shed light on the Victorian era; and Victoria Hislop's work illuminated historical events that I didn't learn much about at school. I also imbibed a great deal from the hefty encyclopedias that my parents bought and from the Internet, both of which I used to complete school projects in the 1990s. They brought knowledge from around the globe to the ends of my fingertips.

Travel is another way for the curious to gain knowledge about other cultures. Personally, I have found that one of the best ways to understand a place is by going there, staying with someone local to the area and soaking in the culture. Over many years, I've gone frequently to Italy to stay with one of my closest friends and her family. By spending so much time with an Italian family, I've become immersed in the culture, close to the people and it cultivated in me a love for the food.

As we've seen so far, yet another and, arguably, the most powerful way many of us learn about people is through the media. Audio-visual content is an immensely powerful disseminator of ideas, ideals and ideology. Storytelling coupled with images is hugely influential. We don't need to use our imaginations when someone presents us with a complete audio-visual package. TV fills in the blanks.

Once TV sets became generally affordable and could be found in almost every home, television became a game-changer in so many ways. For the first time, we could see images that we would have had to imagine while listening to a radio broadcast or reading a newspaper. There's something about moving two-dimensional images that draws us in. The first televised US presidential debate between John F. Kennedy and Richard Nixon changed politics. Those who heard it on the radio believed there to be one winner; those who watched on TV thought there was another:

It's now common knowledge that without the [USA's] first televised debate . . . Kennedy would never have been president. But beyond securing his presidential career, the 60-minute duel between the handsome Irish-American senator and Vice President Richard Nixon fundamentally altered political campaigns, television media and America's political history. 'It's one of those unusual points on the timeline of history where you can say things changed very dramatically – in this case, in a single night,' says Alan Schroeder, a media historian and associate professor at Northeastern University, who authored the book, *Presidential Debates: Forty Years of High-Risk TV*.[8]

TV has long been a powerful tool for encouraging people to make certain choices; that's why TV advertisements are the most expensive, and why TV news and media have become so powerful in driving narratives. Once media professionals began to understand and harness that power, fake news began to proliferate, purveying not only one person's (an editor's) world view but also, at times, intentionally manipulative storytelling, including propaganda.

It's time for a different kind of thinking

I keep returning to the belief that the intent of newsmakers is to inform and not to divide: Perhaps I'm far too pragmatic in the face of contrary evidence. I also believe that the only way we can break out of holding unquestioning beliefs is to do our own research: there's simply no other way. We can choose not to allow someone else's point of view to become our own.

I was brought up to resist groupthink, so I have to try not to be completely contrary much of the time. Objection for the sake of it – just to be seen as a thinker who swims against the tide – is not attractive, especially because groupthinking might be right as well as wrong. In its most positive form, resisting groupthink requires the courage to hold an unpopular opinion when necessary, and such a stance has to be rooted in some kind of reality and good sense. We must be willing to give voice to our beliefs, especially at a time when extreme views are being aired. Those who are more conciliatory should speak but often don't. I dare to believe that this group of moderates is actually the quiet majority.

Conversely, those who have extreme views tend to be very vocal. They know a lot about their narrow interests, and the more they know about a little, the larger their blind spots. Many of these determined commentators seldom allow any space for the notion that they might be wrong. Their singular stories will not allow them to be mistaken; their position is entrenched. News outlets and media organizations carry this bias and intransigent thinking, too, whether or not it's intended.

If media professionals were to produce truly unbiased commentaries, they would have to give what they believed to be untrue as much air time as what they believed to be true. However, the lack of ability by the media to police themselves and ensure such impartiality is revealed by the rules surrounding the run up to UK general elections and referendums. These rules are dictated by the government's Office of Communications (Ofcom). If the media were fair all the time, such stringent measures wouldn't be needed.

In newsrooms, during elections and referendums, time and human resources are dedicated to logging the number of minutes and seconds given on air to each party. When these time slots aren't adhered to rigidly, political-party representatives will complain, as they are keeping tabs too. The newsroom staff are then required to check whether they have abided by Ofcom's rules, some of which are as follows:

Rule 6.2

Due weight must be given to the coverage of parties and independent candidates during the election period. In determining the appropriate level of coverage to be given to parties and independent candidates, broadcasters must take into account evidence of past electoral support and/or current support. Broadcasters must also consider giving appropriate coverage to parties and independent candidates with significant views and perspectives.

Rule 6.3

Due weight must be given to designated organisations in coverage during the referendum period. Broadcasters must also consider giving appropriate coverage to other permitted participants with significant views and perspectives.

Rule 6.9

If a candidate takes part in an item about his/her particular constituency, or electoral area, then broadcasters must offer the opportunity to take part in such items to all candidates within the constituency or electoral area representing parties with previous significant electoral support or where there is evidence of signif-icant current support. This also applies to independent candidates. However, if a candidate refuses or is unable to participate, the item may nevertheless go ahead.[9]

These points are only a portion of the rules; they come with further guidance, including an expansion of what it means to give equal or 'due weight'.

Giving equal weight is not only about fairly dividing the available time; it's also about presenting different views, which the coverage of Brexit exemplifies. For instance, let's consider the claim that, after leaving the European Union (EU), the UK would recover control of £350 million a week. Even if that statement wasn't believed by journalists at the time, the UK's approach to minimizing political bias meant that it was reported as seriously as any other claim. A case brought to the High Court against Boris Johnson, for misconduct in office over the claim, was thrown out. However, fact-checking revealed it was untrue that the UK would rake back £350 million a week. Corrections and apologies are not usually given the same amount of exposure as mistakes, which, as a result, remain uncorrected in most people's minds. And, because this erroneous message was advertised on the sides of buses and in targeted social-media advertisements, it seeped into the public consciousness.

It can be hard to undo the harm caused by the news when, at the time, it's not placed in the correct context – sometimes because of the rules – and therefore not challenged. With regard to minorities, the contextual challenge is often not there. It is hard to ignore the fact that people's individual bias plays a part in such misreporting. At times, I admit, I have written stories that, although within professional guidelines, were shaped according to the way I see the world.

In audio-visual media, as we have seen, bias is revealed through the language used, the clips chosen and the ways they are arranged. Both organizational bias and individual bias affect a story. Therefore, we should be wary and question the narratives we receive. Nevertheless, even with declining trust in the truthfulness of news reporting, the old default setting kicks in for many people; we are likely to believe what we are told on the news that we agree with. We also shouldn't underestimate the loyalty viewers have for familiar newsreaders, whom they see in their own living rooms day after day. The relationship is not one way, even if the conversation is; many presenters build rapport with their audiences by conveying warmth, seriousness and respectability.

Social media add another layer: we become familiar with these journalists outside work, which makes them more human and trust-worthy or, occasionally, the opposite. We prefer not to believe that a familiar individual or news organization would lie. Of course, the journalists wouldn't call it lying; they would say that they have crafted the story to help us to see the truth, to make it easier to understand and to make the complicated simple. When we consider that large and complex topics are now routinely discussed in under five minutes, is it really possible to do so with integrity and without falling back on well-worn stereotypes and pre-existing opinions?

Anti-groupthink

It is clear that we are in an ethical mess. Is it because people intend evil? Is it that there is neither the time nor the resources to do the right thing? What we do know is that many people are being short-changed by the sources of information they choose. Much of the time, traditional media outlets and social media present little beyond a singular, simplistic and convenient story. When it comes to tackling the lack of integrity and paucity of universal inclusiveness in the news, social media are certainly not the panacea they might have first seemed to be.

Although media organizations usually start out wanting 'to tell the truth', they tend to fall foul of the same old ways of doing things. When new and innovative platforms spring up, their founders want to avoid emulating their large corporate rivals. But, as they grow, they discover that they have to be organized, have a hierarchy and signing-off processes, and be slick, just like the big outlets. In the end, everyone needs to make money, so these changes are inevitable. In addition, people tend to hire others who resemble them; so, instead of expanding to encompass difference, the existing culture becomes entrenched.

Most reasonable managers are happy to be disagreed with on issues that they aren't sensitive about. But when it comes to points of view and values, everyone has an Achilles heel. In the end, editors say what's in and what's out; so, from the outset, rather than implying that they are telling 'the (objective) truth', they could admit they are telling 'their truth' because that is what they deliver and we imbibe.

It's not that we shouldn't trust the news; we should be wary of believing it to be neutral because the news doesn't sprout organically – it is manufactured. To seek a surer path of objective truth and to understand our world in a more holistic way, a healthy approach would be to create our own checks and balances, based on external reality.

3

An unedifying choice

I often wonder who wins when – rather than working on solutions to end social-justice problems in their many guises, we spend time arguing about whom we should help or what we should change. We don't even debate how to prioritize aid. Rather than acknowledging that different individuals feel more or less passionately about different social injustices, we try to convince others that they should be as invested in a specific issue as we are. Instead of focusing on the big picture concerning a particular topic, such as education, we debate on who is worthy of being helped. We fail to highlight the fact that many people need support and to admit that, although we're passionate about a certain topic or group of people, others choose to focus on alternative issues.

Headlines about White working-class boys being left behind in education and being worse off than Black boys create a narrative that fuels animosity between two groups that are disadvantaged in different ways, for different reasons. I am yet to understand why the conversation hasn't moved on to the specific, different types of support that these two groups of young people desperately need. Why do we have to choose between the two? The time, energy and emotion spent arguing why one side is worse off than the other would surely be better spent on a deep and thoughtful examination of why any child is left behind in an education system financed by the taxpayer.

Why aren't we moving away from one-dimensional arguments about the reasons young people carry knives? It isn't simply because their fathers are absent or that their parents aren't employed, although these can be contributing factors. We should look at the varied, rather more nuanced, concerns young people have about their personal safety. We should work out how to address their particular worries in a targeted way that yields results.

We see a similarly mistaken focus replicated in discussions around health care, the jobs market and so on. The choice always seems to be one of whom society believes has the most pain, has been the most disadvantaged and is therefore the most deserving of support and necessary funding. Preferably, the arguments should be constructed along lines that do not pit disadvantaged groups against one another. Offering those who witness the arguments such an unedifying choice is to be avoided because it results in harm and mistrust; it antagonizes everyone and helps no one.

4

A culture of confusion

'If you cyan hear, you muss feel'

I sometimes feel as if time were passing quickly and slowly at the same time. The week begins; it passes. What did I do on Monday? I can't remember; so much has happened and, yet, it's as if it were only yesterday. How is it that the week is already over?

Our collective timekeeping seems to work in this way. The world, our attitudes, our technology and the UK's demographic make-up have all changed so much and continue to do so rapidly. Words and phrases that were fine to use last year are now beyond the pale. Many of us find it difficult to keep up – a fact made worse by the prevailing culture not tolerating certain slip-ups in language use and behaviour. At one level, we can understand why people take this rigorous stance; it can be hard to know whether certain words are said in ignorance or with the intent to offend.

Collectively, we travel more or, when we can't, technology takes us wherever we want to go. We have access to more knowledge than ever about our global village. A quick Internet search can give us almost any answer to any question that we might have. Yet personal and public debates don't reflect this breadth and wealth of information; instead, they are binary. We have to pick sides rather than choose the grey areas that make up much of life: are we pro or anti, or politically left or right? While we should be better at knowing and understanding the nuances of other people's lives, it seems that our ability to do so, despite the riches of the Internet and opportunities for travel, is profoundly withered or non-existent regarding everything from politics to social justice.

Nationalism and populism are on the rise, as is the return to the rhetoric and propaganda reminiscent of the dark days of the world wars, when being other was the worst thing that you could be. We have equality and anti-hate crime laws designed to prevent discrimination, but while the letter of the law is usually followed, the spirit does not seem to have quite caught up. This situation has resulted in the continuation – even the deepening entrenchment – of inequality in society, despite a greater number of open conversations about social injustice. The playing field on which we all live, or try to live, is far from level. We find ourselves in a culture of confusion because the way the world could, and perhaps should be, is not the way it is. The frustration with this state of affairs is never far away from the surface, ready to boil over. History shows that we've been on this merry-go-round before: the cycle of inequality, an eruption of anger around it, protests, promises of change, no change – and so the vicious circle continues.

My mother used to say in patois, 'If you cyan hear, you muss feel,' which usually preceded a smack (perfectly legal in the 1980s). To translate, the phrase means, 'If you can't hear the advice to stop what you're doing, you will have to be shown another way.' Many of us are sure that we don't want to continue to experience or witness the issues of the past; the tiresome circularity of the discussions around systemic injustices emphasizes the feeling and belief that we aren't learning and we don't have any workable solutions. For me, part of the answer is to improve communication. We also need a deeper understanding of where we are culturally; then we can assess effectively how to frame the sort of communication that leads to change.

Are we slow cultural-intelligence learners?

What is confusion? It's a sense of being uncertain, unclear or bewildered. We've been all those things concerning how to bring about actual, long-lasting change. We are stuck. We have to think of new ways to encourage the messages about social injustice to land – in us first and then in others. Could it be that the speed of change does not allow 'cultural intelligence'[1] to evolve at the same rate? Is the problem even one of pace? Because of our deep need to belong and to stay safe from those we perceive as different and dangerous in our rapidly changing world, our concerns often arise from a binary, excluding foundation: who is 'them' and who is 'us'? In the shifting sands of our prevailing culture, this question seems to have become i٠ important.

I often used to be asked the question, 'Where are you from?' (These days, I'm asked it less and less.) It's a question that can be answered on a number of levels. My usual response, even when I think I know where the question is heading, is 'Birmingham'. I was born there and brought up there for most of my teenage life. Usually, a second question follows: 'Yes, but *where* are *you* from?' In reality, I'm being asked about my heritage. My skin colour provokes the question, despite the fact that third- and fourth-generation people of colour are now being born here (and despite the fact that the Black community in Liverpool goes back centuries, and the British-Chinese community that has its roots in Limehouse, east London, is nearly as old). My roots are Jamaican but I was born in the UK; I see myself as Black British. In many senses, I am both Jamaican and British. It is for this reason that the whole 'them and us' question is not straightforward. My place of birth and upbringing and my career choices identify me as belonging to 'us' to many, but not to everyone. The question '*Where* are *you* from' implies that 'you' are not one of 'us'; the fact that my saying 'Birmingham' isn't enough confirms it. For some, the mere fact that my skin colour is different means that I'm other rather than British. If I were White, I doubt that I'd have been asked a subsequent question after I'd given my first answer.

Many people think questioning of this kind is offensive. I'm not sure that it always is. Although we might object to the deep, underlying thinking that does raise the question, it doesn't necessarily make someone racist. Some people are inquisitive and naturally want to know more about others. However, when it comes to those who say, 'Keep Britain British', we can be fairly sure that they are racist because by 'British' they mean 'White British'.

The statement, 'Go back to your own country', doesn't make much sense when addressed to a person born in the same country as the racist saying it. Many of the people caught up in the *Windrush* scandal of 2018 believed themselves to be British until the UK government said they weren't and asked them to leave. They had lived and worked here for several decades, participating in society and the economy, paying taxes and bringing up families. The government's policy showed no grace for any of these contributions. Treating people in such a way is intentional; it doesn't happen overnight and it requires a degree of societal consensus to occur.

Who decides who is 'us'? What are the qualifying features? Who benefits from a them-and-us narrative? In a truly equal society that, nevertheless, possesses rich differences, there can be no 'them' who are disqualified and never considered to belong, even though they have conformed, assimilated, achieved and do all the things 'we' and 'us' do.

Populism and 'them and us'

Populism draws heavily on the them-and-us story. It's not only right-wing rhetoric either, which is what we tend to think when we consider populism. On the left, we hear this same narrative, although the meaning of 'us and them' is slightly different; in this case, it is the ordinary people versus the elite. This definition focuses not only on class, status and money but also often on race, gender and sexuality. Whereas on the right in White majority countries, the them-and-us definition contains fewer categories, which tend to be race, class and money. The UK's unique them-and-us narrative was brought into glaring relief around the issue of its leaving the European Union (EU).

Brexit caused one of the most divisive periods in recent UK history. Interestingly, the right-leaning Brexit campaign used traditionally left-wing rhetoric. The slogan 'Take back control' spoke to White working-class people, who were proclaimed the nation's underdogs. The campaign also depended on stories of elitism as much as it did on fear of immigration. Many people attracted by this narrative were either Labour Party supporters or UK Independence Party (UKIP) supporters.

A message that manages to unite both sides of the political divide will be successful. The core messages peddled by the winning Brexit campaign were on immigration and border control (race); how much was given to the EU annually (money); and a perceived lack of independence and sovereignty in law-making (control). The 'Take back control' narrative paved the way for a significant regression in the use of language and behaviour. It was as if all the progress in equality that the UK had made in the past 50 or 60 years was actually very shallow and easy to reverse.

We were blindsided when the proverbial can of worms that society had been trying to keep shut was aggressively wrenched open. And it all occurred at a time when many of us were preparing to push for greater inclusion.

Perhaps the revelation that racism and inequality had not gone away, but had merely gone underground, was timely and not a bad thing; it's better to know the truth. There were some immediate negative ramifications of this discovery: for all the laws and attempts at integration that made the UK's cosmopolitan cities look good, those who held certain views – which had been silenced from mainstream conversation, but were still bubbling beneath the surface – saw their chance to let their opinions resurface and overflow. For them, the tight political slogan 'Take back control' validated their beliefs that they, as British people, had to take back control of the UK from *all* those considered to be dangerous non-British interlopers.

You don't have to agree with the campaign to know that it was very clever. It hit the bullseye for those who felt that they could no longer recognize their world because of the activities of the EU, the press and big business, and the position of marginalized people. The words and sentiments of the Brexit campaign put a voice to feelings and emotions in a powerful way. Although the campaign's message was for a specific time, its consequences have expanded in ever-widening ripples, such that they have come to affect the lives of many private individuals in society.

To make their message credible, the Brexit 'leave' campaigners had to identify 'them'. It was as if Brexit were being fought along cultural battle lines. When people want to win, they don't usually think about the people who might be affected by what they do. Often, we believe that politicians purposely throw certain groups under the bus. Sadly, I fear that it's often worse; they simply aren't giving any thought to the potential consequences of what they say because they, personally, are unlikely to experience the fallout.

As a communication strategist, I usually advise a client to take big ideas and distil them into something simple and easily digestible that will be great for soundbites and snippets on social media. In the strategist's mind, a person is a voter. All the strategist wants and needs from the individual is his or her vote. The outworking of the Brexit 'leave' campaign's simple, effective message was an increase in race-hate crimes: people wearing clothing that marked them out as different, such as hijabs, were attacked and shouted at; foreigners of all ethnicities felt uncomfortable because their accents were used as proof of their being other. For a lot of us, our worlds started to shrink again after many years of living in a society that seemed to be broadening to encompass us, and that was beginning to allow us to feel safe and valued because far-right ideologies had been banished to the fringes of society. Thanks to Brexit, the extremist views have resurfaced and are now too close for comfort.

I was quite shocked when Birmingham – a city that wears its multicultur-alism on its sleeve – voted to leave the EU. There is a suspicion that a large proportion of those who voted to leave did so as a protest against decades of non-White immigration, and because of their discomfort with settled and integrated diaspora communities. Although, of course, not everyone voted to leave the EU for that reason; many people did so because of financial and sovereignty concerns. Thus it's difficult to define the 'leave' vote as one purely based on the issue of immigration. And the result in Birmingham wasn't exclusively down to the 'leave' voters being White. Although the figures in the table below are from the 2011 census, they indicate Birmingham's ethnic breakdown at the time of the Brexit vote in 2016.

The vote was close but the UK left the EU, and Birmingham definitely wanted out. The referendum result was quite challenging to me and many of my acquaintances and friends in the city. For us, difference was a bastion. We believed that the Brexit campaign's emphasis on immigration and the fact that we were a relatively young city would

A breakdown of ethnicity in Birmingham (2011)

	Birmingham (%)	England (%)
White British	53.1	79.8
Black African and Caribbean	7.2	2.9
South Asian	22.5	5.5

Source: compiled from data in Table QS209, '2011 Census: Ethnic group (detailed), Birmingham compared with national and regional figures', *2011 Census: Key statistics for Birmingham and its constituent areas* (London: Office for National Statistics, 11 December 2012), <www.birmingham.gov.uk/downloads/file/4576/census_2011_ks201_ethnic_groupspdf>, accessed 14 June 2021.

result in the citizens rejecting the campaign's narrative and voting to remain. Nevertheless, when Birmingham's multicultural surface is scratched, we can see the serious racial faultlines that have shaken the city in the past. Riots had occurred in Handsworth in 1981, 1985, 1991, 2005 and 2011, with differing degrees of severity, but all involved issues around race. Some of the disturbances were about relations between the Black community and the police; some concerned grievances between the Black and South Asian communities.

In Birmingham, I found it difficult to be intentional about having friends outside the workplace who weren't Black. It was far harder than in London. Birmingham seems to be a mosaic but London is more of a melting pot. And, as an adult, I was confronted with the blatant reality of Birmingham's systemic racism in a church that I attended. Indeed, I found it interesting that both London and Manchester voted to remain in the EU. It emphasized that Birmingham, unlike London and Manchester (in my opinion), is not a truly cosmopolitan city, although London and Manchester undoubtedly have their own problems. The coalescing along racial lines that occurs in Birmingham is something that has to be addressed, especially because it is a city of so many different cultures.

Increased multiculturalism doesn't mean greater harmony, and it certainly doesn't mean more equality for all. In his book *The Five Dysfunctions of a Team*, Patrick Lencioni refers to false melody rather than true harmony.[2] False melody occurs when individuals refuse to engage in constructive, honest conflict; refraining from telling the truth results in frustration. Finally, when disagreement does arise, it tends to be more destructive because of the passive-aggressive nature of the interaction. I'm sure many people who live alongside one another would prefer to get along, but true understanding and deep relationships seem to elude us. So, what is holding us back?

The fight for fairness for all adds to the general confusion. The lack of progress makes no sense when everyone says they want it. But the (in)action tells a different story. Studies show that, for the past 20 years, populism has been on the rise on the right and the left while, conversely, equality and equity have been declining because of populist rhetoric.[3] We can see this rhetoric – and will continue to see it – damaging or even destroying communities. The language that comes with this societal undercurrent of populism can only be divisive, no matter from which side it emanates. One populist side paints the other as the cause of all the country's sufferings while declaring that it knows best what everyone should do, say and be.

The problem with the populist style of communication is that what's 'best' means different things for different people. We continually engage in circular conversations because we ascribe different meanings to the same language. This incessant war of words sows seeds of discontent; we see the effect of this discontent in the behaviour it stirs up. For a time, there was a sense that many of us were beginning to see others different from ourselves as friends, neighbours or, at least, people whom we could tolerate and relate to politely or even cordially. Now, these 'others' are seen as enemies of progress.

Weaponizing words

One language: several meanings

Our society has not yet reached a consensus on how to disagree well, and it's tearing us apart. We have yet to agree about what to say when we disagree or to understand the difference between disagreeing with others and holding them to account. Terms such as 'woke', 'privilege',[4] 'diversity' and 'unconscious bias' have become loaded and mean different things to different people: they might be explanations; they might be insults. In this binary world, how we understand these terms depends on which side of the fence we choose. So how do we even begin to address the plentiful systemic injustices that hold so many back, in so many ways?

I believe that we begin by considering a shared understanding of language. For a start, we can no longer hide behind the excuse that prejudice or bias is unconscious. Pandora's box is open. We all have to be honest enough to admit that we have a problem (that we all feel tense, even fragile, around this conversation) and we have yet to find a solution so that we can get closer to one. Carrying on the way we are is not the long-term answer. Blind spots, safe chambers and lack of understanding: they all keep us from understanding ourselves and others.

Know thyself

Unconscious (or implicit) bias is a frequently used term tl
have different meanings for different people. Here is a de
psychology website:

> Implicit bias (also called unconscious bias) refers to attitudes and
> beliefs that occur outside of our conscious awareness and control . . .
>
> An implicit bias may run counter to a person's conscious beliefs
> without them realizing it. For example, it is possible to express
> explicit liking of a certain social group or approval of a certain
> action, while simultaneously being biased against that group or
> action on an unconscious level.
>
> Therefore, implicit biases and explicit biases might be different
> for the same person.
>
> It is important to understand that implicit biases can become an
> explicit bias. This occurs when you become consciously aware of
> the prejudices and beliefs you possess. That is, they surface in your
> conscious mind, leading you to choose whether to act on or against
> them.[5]

A common understanding of the language employed in the arena of
social justice is required for things to change. Bias, unconscious or
otherwise, is found not only in the usual suspects; it's in all of us. If we
truly care about the world becoming a more just place, we must examine
ourselves for our own prejudices, which may not be the obvious or usual
ones. We might have an aversion to people who are rich or obese, or to
those who speak with a certain accent. Are our bigotries hiding in plain
sight? When and how are they affecting us and other people? How can
we address them?

It's not enough to name our blind spots or our biases and speak
endlessly about all the ways in which they manifest, which is where
most of us stop. True and lasting progress uses that only as a starting
point. I'm not a big fan of telling people to do the work. It can sound
obnoxious and seems to assume that the people concerned have done
no work. Instead, I'd say that there is work to do. We must do the work
and keep working.

Division, conquest and confusion

Divide and conquer is an effective tactic. Togetherness, shared understanding and common purpose precede progress. In the biblical story of the Tower of Babel, some people who speak a common language decide to build a structure so high that it 'reaches to the heavens, so that we may make a name for ourselves; otherwise we will be scattered over the face of the whole earth' (Genesis 11.4). God sees their plan and decides to disband the work because, if they were to achieve their goal, they would be too powerful – too godlike – and their hubris would know no limits: 'nothing they plan to do will be impossible for them' (verse 6). God confuses their language so that they cannot communicate. The work stops and they are 'scattered . . . over the face of the earth' (verse 9), just as they didn't want to be. Divide and conquer is a successful tactic.

Common understanding achieves great things. Promoting a shared vision is helped by having similar points of reference. A shared understanding of language and context is powerful for moving forwards. However, confusion is what we currently have. Language that has myriad mainly negative meanings creates barriers rather than bridges. I use a word to express something and you respond by using the same word, but we attach different meanings to it. There can be no sensible conversation or way forwards, until we gain an understanding of what we are talking about. We also have to acknowledge that the feelings evoked by an interpretation of a term such as 'privilege' may prevent us from responding positively or with humility. What we think of or feel when we hear a certain word or phrase is what determines our reaction. Added to that, we must learn to examine honestly what we believe about ourselves and our place in the world, so that we can get to the truth. Just because we don't associate ourselves with something doesn't mean that it doesn't apply to us.

If we stop weaponizing words, we can begin to get to the root of how they can help us to understand the issues.

A cold welcome

Imagine if, when the HMT *Empire Windrush* came to the UK from the Caribbean, the contribution of Caribbean people to the war effort had been massively celebrated. Imagine if there had been an avalanche of articles and news clips dedicated to thanking the new arrivals for coming to help to rebuild the country. How different the welcome would have been; how much better the integration. Many of the post-war demographic changes (immigration) happened before people were properly informed of all the facts. Could anyone ever be ready for such changes?

We know that stereotypes help us to sort out the world. They are tools for discerning who is a threat, who is not and who belongs where. This is a throwback to the way our brains have developed.[6] Nevertheless, thanks to science, data and even anecdotal evidence, we know that these stereotypes are not necessarily true or helpful, despite many of us choosing to believe them for decades. As a society, we are struggling to root out these long-held assumptions from our collective subconscious and replace them with informed, accurate ones. It is a hard task.

In life, common understanding informs our behaviour in any situation in which we gather together. For instance, queuing is a way of making sure of first come, first served. Some people, however, know the rules but choose to break them; they will try to push in. If they were to give a good reason for doing so, those in the queue might let them in. However, the individuals who are queuing might object and make them go to the back. In this sort of situation, a typically British way of expressing disapproval is to glare and tut. Every British person I know has a story about queuing which demonstrates that we all understand how to behave in a queue. No one is confused. Join the queue. If we were to visit a culture in which people say 'Get in line!', we might initially be confused by the terminology but we would understand the concept. If we were to come from a culture for which the concept is not as rigid as it is in the UK, we would learn the British way very quickly. Because the concept of queuing is so firmly rooted in people's hearts, minds and language, when a problem arises, it's easy to solve.

We cannot keep hiding behind 'unconscious bias'

When social or demographic change affects society, the associated language and ideas also change, often because of the labels the media frequently use. We've seen plenty of linguistic transitions: we've moved from using phrases such as 'melting pot' ('We're all here together') and 'multicultural' ('We're a lot of different people, living beside one another') to using 'diversity' ('We're different together') and 'inclusion' ('We're different but included'). However, the idea of implementing cultural intelligence during periods of cultural change has not been one that we have thought through enough. It's time for all sides to work to do so, and to establish how to expand the existing culture to encompass difference.

So far, the answer to bringing about smooth cultural change has been thought to be assimilation. However, when British people go abroad, assimilation is something that we tend to shy away from: we like to hear our language spoken and to eat familiar food. How, then, can we expect full assimilation from others? This attitude is a hangover from a former time of European colonial empires; yet it still exists and is at the root of the White superiority complex. No attempt was or has been made to look for original alternatives to assimilation. We need to seek a vision for those alternatives because change requires some shape or form; some structure.

In any relationship, one person cannot set all the terms, decide how the communication works, and what's right and what's wrong – that's a dictatorship. Even those who have been on the receiving end of injustice will be frustrated in their desire for change if they are not willing to compromise on how shared community spaces should look. But we have some way to go before we reach a consensus.

For some, a foundation for reaching such a consensus involves rebuilding community relationships. As new, diverse groups have moved in and out of communities, there has been little in the way of actively and effectively introducing different people into one another's lives in a meaningful way. Affirming welcomes don't just happen. When migrants move into an area, we should ask important questions that identify each of them as more than just members of a faceless group.

- Where are they from? (Not just the country; the region, city, town or village too.)
- What did they do? Were they doctors, nurses or office workers?

- Who's in the family? Children? What are their ages? What do they want to be when they grow up?

These human beings are more than just a nameless group of people. We forget that everyone has hopes and dreams, and that most refugees haven't fled their homes just to scrape by on handouts and menial jobs at the bottom rung of society. They don't tend to leave loved ones and familiarity, and risk their lives in leaky dinghies, merely to eke out an existence in a hostile new country; they often dream of contributing by working hard, starting businesses and buying properties, if the conditions are right.

Often, the cold welcome doesn't allow people time to integrate. Our society requires quick assimilation: it doesn't want to wait. Consider how much time we take to get to know and understand other people who share our spaces. When we're surrounded by those we can't comprehend, we feel vulnerable; it can be terrifying. I know; I've been to places where I can't understand the language. When I've tried to learn a new language, it's been uncomfortable to try to speak it to those who are fluent; they've mocked my accent and continually corrected me. Tolerance can work only for so long; it doesn't take too much to undermine it and make newcomers shrink back to what they know.

We cannot continue to chalk up the excuse of failing – or even refusing – to know one another to unconscious bias. When we are aware of our bias, it has become conscious and even an intentional way of thinking about others.

Does the best person always get the job?

When we are aware of conscious bias, the way we communicate about it is the problem. It is one reason why our society has not evolved with regard to social justice. We have to examine why communication in this area has been so poor and has failed to present the big picture. We see this failing clearly in the world of work.

Where some see the opportunities that a fairer and more open world might offer, others see only threats to their comfort and status. I've lost count of the times I've heard, 'We can't just give someone the job because they are Black/female/working class/disabled. We have to hire the best person.' One has to ask why, more often than not, the people in these categories aren't in high-powered, high-status jobs or even in a position to hire others. The answer is because most managers hire in their own image. Statistically, if all the variables were fair, surely 'the best people for the job' would include representatives from minority communities or disadvantaged backgrounds at the ratio they occur in the population. So why aren't 50 per cent of CEOs in the FTSE 100 women? Why aren't half the members of Parliament and the civil servants in Whitehall women?[7] You could extend these questions to cover minority groups in the UK and, indeed, around the world. In fact, in the past few years, the numbers of women in high-status positions have declined.[8]

There is clearly an obstacle that prevents us all from having equal and fair access. I am not convinced that there are too few capable Black/female/working-class/disabled people in this country to occupy all sectors, levels and aspects of work and life. Affirmative action has been happening for a very long time. In White majority countries, I believe, it has mainly affirmed White men. With little or no competition from *all* available, skilled candidates, they have been seen as 'the best people for the job', and, for an age, no one has seen fit to question that assumption. However, this situation is changing as we increasingly understand diversity *and* that diversity of thought helps us to thrive. The issue is not about what people should do; it's about what they're willing to do. Usually, we don't all feel naturally compelled to do the right thing all the time, even when we know that we should. We have not kept pace with the rate of change. We have been slow to communicate the message of equality and equity in a way that people can receive it.

In a couple of places where I've worked, some colleagues thought that I'd been promoted to tick a diversity box, rather than because I had any talent. In a newsroom, news reading is a coveted position. When I was asked to cover for a newsreader who had taken maternity leave, it was clear that a number of my co-workers believed that they were more deserving of the role. One workmate remarked that I'd been offered the opportunity only because of 'diversity'. On another occasion, at the beginning of my career, I was asked to be the presenter of a new current affairs bulletin. I approached a colleague I respected for advice;

he refused to help me because he believed that it was wrc
been chosen for the role. He added that he was speaking to th
behalf of our fellow and more deserving employees. While t
wanted to increase the appearance of diversity on air, they didn't want to
risk the reputation of the programmes by not taking on the best person
for the job. Some of my former co-workers clearly didn't believe I was
that person. One time, I did speak to a manager and suggest that she
could have done more to prevent such an attitude. 'Like what?' was her
response. I answered that she could have shared with our colleagues the
reasons why I was promoted: my qualifications and experience. I added
that we couldn't expect people to know what we don't tell them. We
should say what the individual brings to the table; why promoting him
or her is a good idea.

When someone runs a community, organization or team, he or she
is not usually affected personally by disagreements at a lower level.
Do directors or managers ask the following questions about their
subordinates?

- What sort of culture is developing between employees who are
  thrown together?
- Is the culture shared?
- Is the culture healthy?

In many cases, the answer to the last two questions is 'Probably not',
especially if employees believe that, for the sake of improving diversity, the
organization won't allow them to progress. When this is the perception,
how welcoming are they likely to be to people who are different? Not very.
To prevent hostility, the bosses have to make it clear how employing and
promoting people from a variety of backgrounds benefits everyone. If
they don't, the rank and file won't understand the intentions behind the
management's decisions. Managers should know their teams well enough
to have an idea of their professional hopes and ambitions, and when and
why they are likely to act out.

The prevalent idea that employees should be left to sink or swim is not
a culturally intelligent strategy. How many entry-level schemes are there
that leak as many people as they bring in? It might be that they stall not

because the recruits don't want the jobs but because the existing culture doesn't want the recruits. Have you ever given someone new the cold-shoulder because you preferred somebody else for the job? There it is. We have to move past this familiar narrative and try a new way that matches the walk with the talk.

Equidistance

Social justice, when seen through a lens of 'them and us', is often not equitable at all. Rather than being an equalizer, it divides further, with 'us' saying to 'them', 'We are helping you, therefore, where can we be but above you?'

There is much in the language and relationship of advocacy that will only ever maintain the distance. It will never close the gap but, rather, keep those 'being helped' subordinate. Sometimes, in our rush to help, those of us helping don't even notice this. We can forget to reflect on what is actually helpful or sustainable in the long term.

Helping someone else always feels good, whether we're advising others or providing life-changing gifts; it is uplifting to know that we can be an answer to someone else's problem. It is particularly affirming when we aren't sure of our own place in the world or, more especially, when other people know what we've done. As a result, some of the justice we see being done can be a performance. It may be that we are active and agitate for the reward of being significant and admired rather than to bring about actual change. This attitude can mean that, when the applause isn't forthcoming, we can lose interest and drop causes, which can make a bad situation worse. A little honest examination of our motives for 'helping' might prevent our hurting people or even using them under the guise of goodness.

In recent years, there has been a backlash against 'poverty porn'. When we take pictures of impoverished people and post them, who benefits? Probably not the subjects of the photos. When I was in Malawi, working for a charity, I took photos of that kind and posted them. The things I saw moved me and I wanted to share them. Was I less well intentioned because I shared (and declared) my 'helping' to the world? Would I be happy if, without my consent, someone were to share publicly a moment at which he or she helped me? I questioned my own motives.

Intention can be discerned from the captioning and framing of images. Drawing attention to a cause is legitimate, but we should consider whether the means of doing so are justified, which is the main aspect to think about when helping or advocating for others. When highlighting an issue, are we truly seeing the people concerned as fully rounded human beings or as a faceless group of those who have needs to be met or a problem to be solved? For us to evolve culturally, we have to recognize that we are all one and we must truly regard every person as equal.

Motives and actions that do not align cause confusion. Those receiving help can be unsure of the helpers' true intentions and may, as a result, call them out for behaving like saviours. At a larger scale, an action can appear to be good but it seems 'off' and, ultimately, no long-term change results. We remain 'us' and they remain 'them', and the gap of injustice remains.

Close the gap: don't mind it

Imagine a world with unclouded judgement; without confusion. It may seem unimaginable, but it should be a 'new normal' to work towards, particularly as this melting-pot of a planet is here to stay. With increased globalization, we have more reasons than ever to seek a fairer world for all; one that is less culturally confused and in which the narratives are more nuanced will be more peaceful than it is currently. Experiencing injustice is hard, as is witnessing it (although in a different way). With regard to others whom we don't know or understand, we lose nothing by admitting that our attitudes and words can fall short; after all, every one of us experiences being human together.

When each of us is courageous enough to scrutinize our own feelings and motives, as well as to endure the scrutiny of others, we will begin to see a shift. We didn't purposely make our culture confused, but that doesn't absolve us from playing an important role in restoring a sense of order. We are in control of nurturing our cultural intelligence, of questioning our motives for choosing whom we help (or not) and how we help them (or not). We can choose to examine our biases and think about how to affirm different kinds of people in specific ways.

The migrations that have resulted in the current demographics around the world are not new phenomena. People moving for land, food and economic security has been occurring for thousands of years. And history shows that some migrants wanted to dominate and rule wherever they landed. (Thankfully, colonialism of that kind is mostly a thing of the past.) Alternatively, the migrants assimilated to the local culture. With the way the world is opening up now, I believe that when people arrive at a new location, they tend to prefer to retain their culture *and* imbibe the local culture. We can and should make space for cultural duality: it's an injustice not to do so.

We should also acknowledge that it isn't always easy to allow society to expand. We should stop turning a blind eye to the fact that people face injustice simply for being themselves. Doing so will, in itself, mean some progress. We should stop pretending that the inability to accept change is always someone else's problem and never ours; we have to accept that we are culpable too. We require more than just tolerating and existing alongside one another, and having little or no interaction; we need a wholehearted acceptance of difference, although it can be difficult to find a common approach to living together. Only by being in relationship with others, and trying to understand them, can we begin to see where the misunderstandings lie.

A survey found that a significant proportion of Britons don't like to hear people speaking foreign languages in in the UK.[9] How interesting. The British are known to be generally monolingual – that is, resistant to learning other languages, particularly as people from many other nations learn to speak English. So, although we expect to be able to speak English abroad (or that could just be me), we dislike it when other people speak their own languages here. We have to examine that arrogance – that root of superiority.

It can take time to establish whether people who aren't like us are good, bad or indifferent. It can sound trite, but disparate groups of people generally have more in common than not. The differences aren't deal-breakers; they aren't bad. Our focus, however, tends to be on the negatives rather than the human hopes, dreams, joys and pains common to us all. The gap of inequality closes when we see humanity in someone else; when we refuse to see another as a human being, the gap between 'them' and 'us' inevitably widens. What we don't attempt to change will simply never happen.

The upside is that we are the solution. Some of us may not have encountered some or any of these inequalities. The fact that we might not have does not mean that these issues are any less real or serious, and are not negatively affecting someone else's existence. Discovering more about how other people experience the world, both negatively and positively, can help us to recognize what a fuller life can mean. It can open our eyes to the part we have to play in making the world more equitable, so that others can know what they should have and could be.

We are confused because we can see that the world should be a better place and yet it's not. We are confused because we have talked so much about the problem and yet have found no solutions. We are confused because we know that there is racism, sexism, classism and many other issues so widespread that they cannot be laid at the door of only a few easily recognizable extremists; yet no one seems to be able to identify the mainstream perpetrators of these behaviours – probably because we don't look inside ourselves. The confusion is the gap between what we know could be, plus the words that confirm it, and the inaction that means we never arrive. If we were to begin to see ourselves as part of the problem, it would mean that our altered behaviour could be part of the solution: we could change and close the gap. Such a move towards action would start to unravel the culture of passivity and expected assimilation, and turn the culture into one that could expand to be welcoming; one of which we could be proud.

5

Where are the
White community leaders?

I have never seen or heard of social commentary from a 'White community leader'. Not from media outlets, in newspapers, magazines or on the radio have I noticed the following said or written: 'And now we'll hear from So-and-So, a White community leader . . .' It's curious because I hear about other kinds of community leader: Black, Asian and so on. It would seem that community leaders are only for those who are othered. It reflects the assumption that White is usual or 'normal' and then there's everything else. It also illustrates the stereo-typing around perceived monolithic otherness – that everyone seen as belonging to a particular group must all be so similar in attitude and culture that a single person can speak for them all. The complete lack of 'White community leaders' reveals an acceptance that not all White people think similarly or behave in similar ways, and that they aren't a monolithic group. This level of nuance and complexity is not offered to other, non-White communities in the UK.

Within the professed Black community, there are various groups without any specific leaders, self-appointed or otherwise. Not all Black people and groups share the same aims or the same hopes and dreams, and we don't necessarily agree on how to achieve those aspirations and goals that we do have in common. In fact, historically, there has been prejudice within the wider Black community: people of African descent and those whose antecedents hail from the Caribbean were (and still can be) at odds.

While prejudice of any type isn't acceptable, it is fine for groups within supposed, monolithic communities to have unique differences. The more that minority groups own their complexity and variety, the sooner others will stop treating us as though we were all the same. With regard

to Black people, different demographic and economic communit
different specific wants and needs, which is why the 'Black and n
ethnic' (BAME) label is problematic. Is there one Black community? Or
are there Black communities? We don't have spokespeople, but people
who choose to speak about the special interests to which they are
aligned. When spokespersons for a cause relating to the working classes
happen to be White, they tend to represent a specific group. They are
not usually asked to represent the White community in general. This
is where we, as Black people have to position ourselves. Yes, as a wider
group, we have similarities and a shared push for equality and equity
but, within that group, various communities act in their own, different
self-interests.

Some people might say that this perception is completely contrary
to all that they see and believe, and that it's wrong. In my opinion, this
decades-old diasporic community has, over time, become organized
according to class, gender and level of education. Our communities
are defined by more than just skin colour. Trying to define the shared
outcomes and goals of the Black community is difficult. Black people
who are on the right politically have very different views about what
our shared goals outcomes should be from those on the left. It harms
Black people as a whole when we ostracize those whose views differ
from ours.

Before I moved to a city with a higher proportion of Black people
than the one where I'd grown up, I hadn't encountered the concept of
not being Black enough. In the new city, people pointed out that I wasn't
very Black because of the way I spoke and behaved. If you're brought up
in a White majority city, you know that when you're Black, you're Black.
Full stop. And when I look at myself in the mirror, I am just Black. This
idea that someone might not be 'Black enough' reveals a belief that all
Black people have to behave and think in certain ways. It exposes the
view that there is a specific ownership of Blackness. I don't think any
one way of being, speaking or thinking can own Blackness; all of us who
are Black own it. When someone is Black, he or she is part of the overall
Black culture.

Just as no one White person can speak for all White people, no single
Black person can speak for us all; we're too complex and disparate. We

must not allow terms (and their misuse) to bind us into a monolithic body, which supposedly has one mind and one way. We should embrace our complexity. We do not behave as though we belong to a monolithic entity; neither should we allow ourselves to be labelled as one.

6

Blind spots

Communication as a tool is our greatest strength if we know how to use it; it is our weakness if we don't. When I think about the interactions we have concerning social justice, I see how they hold us all back, although everyone involved would like the discourse to be more effective. So, why isn't it more effective?

In our relationships with others, we continually reveal things about ourselves, whether or not we verbally communicate those things. I think many of us are very good at spotting how *other* people might improve their communication and action. But how can *we ourselves* make more of an impact? What if we were all to admit that none of us has a fully formed, correct view about everything? Wouldn't it help each of us to recognize the humanity in ourselves and others? Our blindness to our own shortcomings, coupled with failing to recognize that others are human and err, causes these conversations to be very difficult. How can we see ourselves in a way that is truthful so that we might see others more truthfully? If we genuinely want to find solutions to very serious problems, we are going to have to communicate in new ways. As we communicate, we must bear in mind that change is possible. We must also be willing to change our methods when they don't work or produce results.

A kink

Most of us don't know when we're wrong, which is a real kink in the human psyche. We can spot danger; our bodies regulate themselves in amazing ways; and we've managed to find cures for many ailments. But we fail to notice when we persist strongly in going down the wrong path. There are some truths that we just cannot see. We are like children who put their shoes on themselves, but on the wrong feet. They will not be persuaded that they must be uncomfortable because they are proud of their achievement and are adamant that their feet are fine.

In a twist that could be considered either cruel or kind, that kink in the human psyche allows us to feel good about the decisions we make, even when we're wrong. We are able to be proud of who, and what, we think we are. However, with genuine, concerted self-reflection and awareness, we can begin to make honest assessments of who we are and why we make the decisions we do. For most of us who lead busy lives, it's hard to monitor our thoughts and behaviour continually, so we usually return to our default settings.

Many of us have felt the influence of this kink. There are times when we are sure we are correct about an issue but someone else tells us we're not. We swing between these two positions and we begin to feel uncertain. Underneath those layers of uncertainty, most of us think of ourselves as good and reasonable people much of the time. We usually think of those moments when we are neither good nor reasonable as being the fault of someone or something else out of our control, particularly when the incident or situation is extremely negative. The misplaced confidence that we have in our being good or reasonable carries us a long way. However, at times, that confidence will be squashed by irrefutable facts or by someone who has a clearer view of a situation or story than us, and then we have to accept that we are not always right. Even so, in many cases, we can't or won't see that we are wrong; this kink is our blind spot.

Blindness

Blindness is the absence of seeing. With regard to social justice, we cannot address what we can't see or don't want to see.

We all have a physical blind spot at the back of each of our eyes. The blind spot blots out an area of our sight but, most of the time, we're not aware of it. Interestingly, we can see all around the blind spot, just not the area affected by the spot itself.

Not only do we have physiological blind spots; we also have psychological ones. Our blind spots help us to feel secure about what we think and how we behave towards others. Whether it's wilful or we can't help it, our ignorance around issues of social justice gives us the false sense of security that we're doing the best we can. It's easier to see someone else's blind spot than our own, which helps us to feel better about ourselves. If we were truly honest, we would have to admit that we were being unjust to others when we do so. We have to be able to acknowledge that we cannot see everything; it's impossible. We always miss something, and this very human failing is a barrier to the common understanding that might lead to change or even just improved dialogue.

The good news is that there are ways to overcome our blind spots and compensate for our lack of vision. Obviously, no one can see out of the back of his or her head (except mothers, of course). Only having forward vision is what makes driving so dangerous. There's a lot on the road that we can't see. While I was learning to drive, a dear elderly lady at church said, 'You have to remember to drive safely for yourself and for others.' That dampened my excitement somewhat. Of course, I knew that mine wasn't going to be the only car on the road. I simply hadn't considered that other drivers might not be driving safely or see my car coming. All I was thinking about was the joy of being independent on the road. The realization that I would have to be continually alert for the potential errors of other drivers seemed a huge responsibility. Nevertheless, as I learned to control my car, I became increasingly competent at being aware of what was around me and the things that I had to anticipate when I had no clear view. Also, driving involves using tools, such as mirrors, to help with observing conditions. We can see much more with the aid of the mirrors than without; they help us to notice what would otherwise go unseen: we can see vehicles speeding up from behind, for example. Even then, there are still blind spots, such as the one over the driver's shoulder.

We can be wrong about many things, yet we often enter conversations about justice as if we had a clear, 360-degree view of the issue. Nevertheless, there are some things hidden from view. Our limited knowledge doesn't mean that we should reign in our passion when stating our case. Rather, we should enter the dialogue humbly aware of what we don't or can't know, and that there might be aspects and factors that we haven't even begun to consider.

Mirrors

Some of my close friends and family could be said to be like car mirrors. I believe it to be a wise strategy to surround myself with people who are not like me to be those mirrors.

They bring into the picture the factors that I can't or won't see and, sometimes, I reveal to them what they've missed. They show me when my thinking and actions are wrong, which gives me a new perspective. When one of my blind spots is exposed, it may be a tough way to learn but I do so and I get better. Although having our faults pointed out to us is usually unwelcome, it is necessary for our personal growth and improvement. It is enriching to gain other perspectives. This is one of the reasons that our relationships are so important – although societal change might start with one person, it is rarely, if ever, completed by only one.

We have to be willing to be open to correction, and others have to be willing to be corrected. We must also acknowledge that we all may have missed certain factors or aspects of the issue to be addressed. That acknowledgement of blind spots could be a vital part of finding solutions, but I've yet to see people take that on board. I've often noticed a certain blindness in myself, particularly when I'm convinced of something. I tend to know a lot about a small area of a subject but not a lot about it generally. And the bit I do know gives me a false sense of security (and superiority) – a little knowledge can be a dangerous thing.

The more we are exposed to the information that we don't know – the bit that we can't see – the more we should consider what else we might have overlooked. It seems to me that when the discourse turns to those areas about which we're less sure, we're likely to shut down the conversation and retreat to a safe chamber of familiar knowledge. However, exposure to things that we haven't thought of can take us on a journey of discovery, but only if we want to know more and expand our knowledge. Most of the time, in our blindness, we don't want to. We choose, instead, to halt a conversation that could lead to change, precisely because it shows us what we don't know, which in itself makes us uncomfortable.

Being a Black woman: the caveat

I'm a Black woman, so I know a great deal about being Black and a woman; after all, I have lived and I am living the experience. But within the wider group of Black women, there are millions of people who have lived millions of different lives. My intimate knowledge of my own experience could lead me to believe that I know and understand others' experiences more intimately than I do. Such a misapprehension would result in my having inaccurate assumptions about all other Black people and all women. For instance, I might believe that they would all come to similar conclusions about certain situations and deal with them in the same way that I would. I might even be arrogant enough to think that I could speak for all Black women. Have you ever generalized about a group to which you belong, only to realize that your view was far from the reality? That blind spot is one we often miss.

We might have a reasonably comprehensive view of something and yet miss some very important facts. Other people are not us and we are not them. Although we will have things in common, the variables are innumerable. How many times have you heard someone speak on behalf of a group – to which you supposedly belong – and you've thought, 'I really don't agree. He or she doesn't speak for me'? Self-appointed spokespeople often not only have access to a microphone but also possess a massive blind spot. They rarely have detailed knowledge of all those for whom they claim to speak. If they did, they would know that there is a great deal they haven't taken into account and they would qualify much of what they share.

Those who are truly in touch with others, and who understand their own fallibility, tend to acknowledge the caveats. Rather than acting as go-betweens, filtering opinion and deciding who may or may not have access to media and public platforms, they will provide opportunities to build communication with a wider section of the group to gather a variety of viewpoints. They admit what they can't see and don't know because they want to seek solutions rather than be considered oracles – the ones who know everything.

Our experiences of the situations and people close to us are deeper and more intimate than our knowledge of the world in general, which is usual. Because of this, we have to recognize when we need mirrors so that we can be truly helpful in communicating for others and ourselves. We must also learn to recognize the impact of assuming to speak for others and of denying them the opportunity to speak for themselves. We don't know what we don't know, and we will continue not to know without intervention.

It could be argued that, as long as I'm speaking for Black women, I'm helping, so what does it matter if I don't know everything about every single Black woman? It would matter less if I were to lay out the caveats and qualify what I said by admitting that I was speaking for myself and others to whom I'm close. I would also have to admit that there was a vast range of experiences about which I couldn't comment.

In some general ways, speaking up for the wider group is the right thing to do but we must be self-aware when doing so. We must acknowledge that there's much we're ignorant about, including topics that we think we know well. What we communicate might not be the full picture but the way in which we communicate can carry a humility that is helpful for the wider dialogue.

'Authenticity' is an overused word but we need more of it in the discourse surrounding social-justice issues. People can often spot phoneys and weak, underdeveloped arguments, which they will use as an excuse to dismiss or prevent further conversations. Lack of authenticity, therefore, is a block to progress. It is, however, one that we can remedy, but only with openness, honesty and by not being afraid of admitting our limitations.

Until it happens to you

Sweeping generalizations are easy – but unwise – to make. Yet we make them all the time without querying or questioning why we do. The things I want to change are the things I can no longer accept, not those I believe to be tolerable. Most people change their position when they are presented with evidence that touches their minds and hearts. In other words, the change starts with seeing or experiencing something first-hand. For instance, many people will routinely walk by someone shaking a bucket for a cancer charity – until, that is, a friend or relative develops cancer; then they are more likely to stop to put some money in the bucket. Centring yourself to try to understand the problem from the clearest point of view you can have – yours – is a shared human trait. This phenomenon could, instead, be termed the proximity or personalization of a problem. As Bryan Stevenson, the founder and executive director of the Equal Justice Initiative, says, 'When you try to problem-solve from a distance you miss the details.'[1] This attitude directly contradicts the loud call of some liberals: 'Don't centre yourself!'

Empathizing with others in their circumstances is no bad thing. When a celebrity dies, there is usually a mass outpouring of grief. Those mourning the celebrity's loss won't have known him or her personally, but they would have been touched by the individual's work or other positive aspects of his or her public life. Not knowing the celebrity personally doesn't make the outpouring of grief wrong or any less authentic. Others who didn't particularly admire the celebrity, however, may feel little about the death, although they might acknowledge that it's sad. When a problem is abstract and has little or nothing to do with us personally, our reaction or impetus to do something tends to be slight.

We see things one way until our blindness is removed and we realize that what seemed so straightforward is rather more complex. What isn't seen can't be addressed but what we do see might provoke us to act. Sometimes, it's helpful to try to become more invested in an issue and to make the effort to know and empathize with those involved, but we have to think about how to implement that behaviour publicly. Placing ourselves in a position in which we personalize another person's problems doesn't mean that we dismiss their experiences and pain, or displace or 'de-centre' them in any way, and it shouldn't.

Marcus Rashford

The footballer Marcus Rashford has been praised for highlighting child food poverty in the UK and for taking concrete action to address it. His passion comes directly from his own experience of growing up in a household without enough money or food. His position as a well-known sportsman has given him a huge platform from which to alert the whole of the UK to this severe, appalling inequality, while his intimate understanding of what it is to be poor and hungry means he has done so with authentic authority.

To help those who were unaffected by the issue (and so weren't able to care) to relate to those in the midst of it, Marcus Rashford told us about his own childhood. He didn't claim to speak for all children. Rather, he spoke about what he knew – the issue of poverty and child hunger – and laid out solutions. He made things happen. He brought people with him because he was truly a bridge between those who were unaware of the issue and those who were suffering because of it. He educated more than he agitated. And he focused on solutions rather than theories.

Worlds within a world

Culture and other identifiers help us to understand the world. But to rely on them solely is to try to wear one size that definitely doesn't fit all.

If we were to take a family, it could be large or small (it doesn't matter which), the range of opinions, ideas and lifestyles within it would provide a glimpse of the wider world. My dad has ten siblings; so ours is a large family, spanning three continents, that includes more than 30 grand-children and between 40 and 50 great-grandchildren. Despite the fact that we are all descended from John and Iona Aldred, we are not alike. There are some similarities with regard to genetics, personality types and the views we hold about certain issues. Beyond that, there are quite a few things that we do not see in the same way. The idea that I could possibly represent fairly all the disparate views of my entire family would be a huge blind spot; you couldn't ascribe to me all the beliefs of one of my uncles, nor mine to him. We are individuals who happen to be part of the Aldred family.

There is, nevertheless, an invisible glue that holds families together: a sense of belonging, understanding and loyalty, despite many differences. So it is within cultural groups. Just as we tend to defend our families no matter what, in our communities, we may defend what outsiders might consider to be indefensible. We can be willingly blind to the wrongs committed by those with whom we share some kind of commonality. It can be expedient to ignore elements that might hinder our achieving important, shared goals.

As the diversity of experiences and views within one family shows, it can't be possible for the stereotyping of whole genders, cultures and so on to hit the mark every time, if at all. Those who think in terms of singular narratives are, more often than not, missing the mark. There's so much we don't see because we don't know, and we fail to communicate with the aim of investigating further.

Partial sight

I don't pretend to have written this book as someone who has fully rounded vision and who is waiting for everyone else to catch up. I wrote it because I want to explore how our lack of honest communication prevents progress.

I want to think about how we all perpetuate injustice in its various guises while also suffering because of it. Few people are free from being both perpetrators and victims. While the injustices vary, affecting our lives differently, our common humanity is the cause of most of them. When we acknowledge the potential for injustice inside ourselves, too, we can begin to move towards ending it. When we can be honest with ourselves, we can be honest with one another and begin to communicate effectively to reach lasting solutions.

I'm someone who has blind spots, which you've probably identified as you've read this book. My blinkers are a product of the life I've lived: my parents, my family, my experiences and everyone I've met have helped to contribute to how I see – or don't see – the world. The variables affecting my point of view are innumerable. How about you? How did you create the last sentence you spoke? Who taught you each word of it? You probably can't remember; yet you've learnt words in isolation; you've learnt groups of words from books, films and conversations. You've formed sentences, coalescing words acquired from various sources. But there are still lots of words that you don't know and which you may never learn.

I've chosen to write this book from a place of admitting my limitations. All I can share is my understanding, based on what I've seen, heard and experienced. What I write has to come with that honesty. I'm not an academic or a scientist; I'm someone who observes how we use the tools of communication, and I want to examine how we might use them with greater skill.

Here is what I've noticed about the world, and I'd like to suggest what might help us to move forward. While working in the media for more than a decade, I observed so much about the way people communicate. I learnt a great deal about the messages behind the messages; how slight, barely discernible linguistic biases in communication could shift attitudes over time. I saw how and why some messages seemed to cut through the noise and others didn't. I witnessed how personal agendas became public ones.

After I left broadcasting, I saw a very different side to communication – how ineffective it can be at times; how people, while trying to do good, don't notice their biases and prejudices – to harmful effect. I discovered how much of a role personal agency plays in what is said and by whom, and who has a say and who doesn't.

I love politics and watch election cycles and campaigns with great interest. I've seen that certain messages trickle down to affect how people feel about and behave towards one another. I was an early adopter of social media and have observed them turn into what they are today; I've noticed how interactions have evolved over time to become angrier and increasingly binary and divisive. In all this, the common thread is that we no longer (if we ever did) communicate in a way that will bring change. We are more interested in being heard – even more, perhaps – than in being understood.

Personally, I want to see change rather than just hope for it. I believe that if we were to change the way we communicate, if we were willing to accept that people and narratives are complex, we would witness the change for which we long in many areas.

My family, church and school

My father was a minister until I reached my early teens. We moved a lot because of his job, and so my younger sister and I went to seven different schools. I learnt a great deal about people from going to the south of the country, to the north and then back to the Midlands, where I was born. I discovered how different British people are, depending on the region in which they lived. In Sheffield, when I was on the way to school, most adults would say good morning to me as I passed them on the road. In Birmingham, not so much. I live in London now; how likely is it that people will say good morning to me on the street there?

When I was younger, my family lived in cities populated mostly by White people, and then more diverse ones as I got older. We encountered different accents and groups. Back in those days, it was all snail mail, so we didn't have the time to write to existing friends as we were making new ones; I learnt early on how to start over and leave the old behind. Despite the number of times we moved, there were some things that stayed the same throughout my childhood: the family unit, being part of a Black majority church and my huge love of reading.

Even now, I find changing aspects of my life relatively easy, although it can be emotionally tough. I took a psychometric test a couple of years ago. I demonstrated an above average tolerance for change, which I put down to the experiences of my formative years. What we experience when our characters are still forming tends to dictate how we'll react to events and situations as adults.

Seeing

I didn't see my parents argue until I was about 13. It was such a surprise when it happened that I thought they might get divorced. I'd seen other couples argue before, but not my parents.

There is a certain amount of stability and confidence that comes when there are no perceived holes in the family boat. I have two sisters, and my parents encouraged all of us to speak our minds. We had family meetings during which we could discuss how we felt about things. (As there were three girls, you can understand that there was often an abundance of tears during those get-togethers.) From those opportunities to share freely, we received a couple of important messages.

First, we understood that we would be heard and that what we had to say mattered. Of course, as we grew older this sharing of opinions became slightly problematic; we thought absolutely everything was up for discussion with our parents when it wasn't.

My parents' style of parenting was deliberately different from the parenting they'd received. Both Mum and Dad were born in Jamaica. Mum came to the UK as a child and Dad as a teenager. They had both spent periods of time living away from their parents for various reasons – the main one being the migration of my grandparents to England. My grandparents, like many others of their generation, left their children in Jamaica until they had settled and were in a position to send for them.

My sisters and I were brought up with conservative Jamaican and Christian values. There was no swearing or speaking slang. No music or TV music channels were allowed on in the house. Of course, during the holidays we would be allowed to watch TV, but we would quickly switch over from a music channel called The Box to something else when we heard Dad coming in through the front door. From around the age of 11, we were taught to cook: it was proper cooking – Caribbean Sunday dinners with all the trimmings, including Guinness punch, a Jamaican treat. We washed our own school uniforms and ironed them. Mum wanted us to be independent and we were. It was different then; parents would leave their children alone more. We played out on the swings that Dad got us. We went to church – a lot; that was our number-one desti-nation. By we, I mean my younger sister and me; our eldest sister is five years older than I am and, by the time I was prepubescent, she was doing her own thing.

The second important message we received from those family meetings was about groupthink. Dad was anti-groupthink and believed in perpetual excellence, which was painful when it came to school results. He told us that, when we went to church, we shouldn't leave our brains at the door, even though he was the pastor.

Church and belonging

Church played a huge part in our lives; we spent a great deal of time there. After school, we would often go to church when Dad was working. Many of our close family friends also attended our church, which was part of a denomination called the Church of God of Prophecy. Originally founded in the USA by White American Christians, it was planted in Jamaica and brought to the UK by the *Windrush* generation. It had congregations all across the UK, which was why we moved so much. Even when we lived in very White cities, church was a very Black space. Historically, culturally, spiritually and musically our Blackness was affirmed. It was who we were. We had members who were there from the cradle to the grave. There were older people who still had their Jamaican accents and younger people who spoke the local English dialect. The life we led, especially in Sheffield, when we were a bit older, was very different from that of our White schoolmates. But our difference didn't matter much or affect who we were. Our Blackness was never questioned by us. We were proud of our identity and never wanted to be anything else.

A love of reading

Alongside these formative experiences of family and church community was my love of reading. I was four years old when my elder sister taught me to read. I was very keen and began to read anything and everything. Between six and seven years of age, I started to scan newspapers. In my class at school, I was always ahead in the reading stages. At home, I read Martin Luther King and Malcolm X, as well as Shakespeare, the *Reader's Digest* and any novels that lay to hand. I was also a quick reader – I read the Bible right the way through a couple of times. From the public and school libraries, I borrowed books by Gwen Grant and Roald Dahl; I had diverse tastes and enjoyed the feeling of being transported to other worlds. I would embarrass my sisters on the school bus as I laughed to myself while immersed in a book.

Culture shock

Our formative years shape the way we see and interact with the world. We cannot underestimate the strength of the views we form, up to the age of five, about who we think we are – until something or someone teaches us otherwise.

My family's move to Birmingham when I was 13 was a massive culture shock for me. Before we left Sheffield, I was sad at the thought of leaving my friends but looked forward to living in a city where a greater number of people looked like me. The national headquarters of our Pentecostal church was in Birmingham and more of our extended family was there too.

Then we arrived. School was a disaster for me. My Sheffield accent wasn't accepted and, to make it worse, owing to an administrative error – by Dad – we didn't go to the best school. We went from attending a

Sheffield Catholic school that had strict rules most people followed – and where many children had a faith background and came from families similar to ours – to an inner-city school where we had little in common with most of the kids. It was at that school that I was introduced to the concept of not being Black enough.

To my knowledge, out of all the parents of the 400 pupils at the school, my parents were the only ones who were married. Books weren't cool, neither was being in the top set or putting your hand up in class too much. There were about only five children in the whole school who weren't on free school meals. My sister and I were two of them. That's when I realized that much I had assumed, because of how my family lived, wasn't always true for others. At 13, this realization was something I absorbed subliminally, intuitively, which made what I was beginning to understand difficult to articulate.

All that I had understood about being female and Black did not fit with what I was now seeing and hearing. They were at odds with what I was supposed to desire and do. My parents' values were different: they might not have been into buying the latest trainers but they owned their own home.

At 13, this is what I witnessed. It was all so strange and it didn't make sense.

Middle-class Black people

The move to Birmingham revealed all these blind spots of which I had been unaware. Prior to our returning there, 95 per cent of the Black people my family knew were Christians who had similar values to ours. My sister once pointed out that it was in Birmingham we first heard about benefits and council housing. Even if we had known people who lived in council housing, we weren't aware of it. In other cities and churches, most of those we knew comprised two-parent families who lived in their own homes. Black churches would often decry education over spirituality from the pulpit; nevertheless, doing well in school was encouraged. Buying a house was encouraged. Our part of the diaspora community believed in God for provision and also worked very hard for all we had. We thought that all Black people lived the way we did.

I was brought up with this singular story and I believed it. But then came Birmingham and I was no longer sure. 'Am I Black enough?', I wondered. At that time, without the ability to articulate how I felt about being exposed to the gap in my knowledge, I communicated it in a different way. I spent a lot of time at the nurse's sick station, waiting for my parents to collect me from school. This was partly because of the unkindness of other children and partly owing to my refusal to assimilate (which I still sometimes do). Thankfully, for my younger sister and me, our time at that school came to a premature end. One day, when Dad picked us up, he saw schoolchildren brazenly smoking weed at the school gates. (I'd never even smelt weed before going there.) We were promptly sent somewhere else that had a more familiar culture.

My parents weren't moved by histrionics. My mother's view was that she didn't send me to school to make friends; she sent me there to learn. She didn't wait each day to hear whether or how I was getting along with people. As far as she was concerned, any friend I gained should be considered a bonus. In fact, this (cultural) attitude is one that I carry to work. Others might consider that, because I seldom, if ever, join in, it means that I'm shy or stuck up. They might not stop to think that I was brought up to focus on learning and achieving, and that I see the working environment in a similar way and not as a social space.

Establishing where someone comes from can shed light on his or her way of interacting with us. There's often something we just can't see. All we are aware of is the behaviour emanating from their experience. It's not easy to articulate all the things that make us who we are, and many of us don't always make the connection to the state of our current relationships. In a busy world, we often skim the surface of our feelings, thoughts, issues and situations. When it comes to others, it's much simpler to take the superficial, wedge it into a stereotype and give it little thought.

It's all complex

Connecting the dots is not straightforward. When we start to do so, it becomes complex, which dissuades many of us from exploring further.

Rather than being put off by the current discourse around change, we should ask, 'If the world is not what I think it is, where have I been all this time? As society and culture change and move, who am I? What does change say about me, about us, about the people I love? What does it say about the people I don't like very much?'

When we feel small in the face of big issues and injustice, many of us sit at a metaphorical nurse's sick station, hoping to avoid changing parts of ourselves, which would feel like a definite loss. And we do so despite knowing that the status quo has to change. Do we even have the energy to try to make a difference? When we see injustice and feel helpless or hopeless, and choose to do nothing, it challenges our view of ourselves as good and reasonable people. Do we do nothing about a problem because of cultural blindness or do we do nothing because we've glimpsed the issue and that's more than enough? Perhaps we do nothing because, although we want change, we want it without sacrifice – without the risk of losing relationships, influence and opportunities. Perhaps we just prefer to live in ignorant bliss. How can we articulate the truth about how we feel without seeming selfish or self-serving? Not easily. Yet, the path of ease is what most humans want. We want to be loved and liked; speaking up for change doesn't usually result in popularity – unless everyone already agrees; if they do, it's probably because we aren't advocating for anything much at all.

Truth

We all hold personal beliefs to be truths, including those about the ways we see ourselves and the world. The moment our truths begin to unravel, the ground beneath our feet becomes shaky. That's why we hold on to familiar ways of seeing things: the way we are and the reasons why. Facing the unfamiliar can be challenging, particularly when it requires us to look at our own attitudes and behaviour; we fear that what we might discover won't be attractive. Because of this fear, many of us feel tense when we enter conversations concerning social issues. We fear that we might have to be the ones to change. As a result, the interactions can become heated because we believe that not only is our point of view being questioned but so, too, is our very being – *who* we are. In reality, what is being questioned is who we *believe* ourselves to be. Many of us don't easily separate *who* we are from who we *think* we are, which makes change difficult.

When it is put to us that we may hold prejudiced views, we don't tend to want to believe so, let alone admit it, especially publicly. Privately, we can ask ourselves questions: 'Am I prejudiced? Am I a bad person or do I just hold some dodgy views? How can I find out without doing myself a disservice and looking bad to those around me, whose opinions I value?' But we can't gain a greater understanding without exposing ourselves in some way. Sadly, instead, many of us have chosen to continue to have unedifying conversations publicly in preference to examining ourselves and changing.

We want others to do the work of changing

When you're about to enter a tense conversation, it's as if your whole body were feeling it. Tension builds around discourse when people don't agree and they know it; the more urgent the need for a resolution, the greater the tension.

We have our blind spots; we have our non-negotiables; we also have no intention of changing our minds. Each person is thinking, 'Someone is going to have to give way, but it won't be me.' No one wants to be the individual who backs down and changes, especially as most of us think we're reasonable people who have reasonable views. Rather, we want to make those on the other side of the conversation accept that we are reasonable and right, and, crucially, see things our way. It is this attitude that results in tension.

We all understand that it is quite difficult to change someone's mind; nevertheless, it's the starting point for many of us in conversations around social justice, no matter which side of an argument we're on. We all seem to assume that we have to change others: their behaviour and their minds. No wonder – when we have both (or more) sides starting from such an immovable position – we don't reach agreements and find solutions. Rather than communicating to be understood, we communicate to dominate.

Most of us go into many of our exchanges convinced of our rightness before the other person has even spoken. We 'know' what he or she is going to say and we're convinced that he or she is wrong. If we weren't sure, there would be more at stake. Our personal truth, pride and view of ourselves are on the line, so we believe we must hold firm. We see this attitude increasingly in the new town squares that are online platforms.

I don't think social media, in and of themselves, are the biggest problem. Unfortunately, the people who run the platforms have grasped how humans tick. They have 'hacked' our underlying behaviours. They have tapped into who we *really* are rather than who we *think* we are, just so that we'll stay on their sites for longer. As a result, we feel safe to indulge some of our less pleasant tendencies. The safer we feel over time about giving in to those tendencies, the less inhibited we become about increasingly revealing them. Human beings have always had questionable inclinations but, prior to the advent of social media, our communications reached far fewer people, which made it harder to find those who held similar views. Social media have merely made echo chambers easier to find.

Echo chambers are nothing new, although they are now in plain view, exposing our thoughts for many, many more people to see. Of course, most of us like to think that it's everyone else who behaves badly on social media platforms – not us. But, of course, we don't just sit in traffic; we are traffic.

These spaces are where we start what we hope will be society-changing conversations. We make the mistake of trying to have tough exchanges on platforms that are built only for a shallow level of connection, and aren't suitable for nuanced discussions. Not only that, as with other areas of life that are played out online, power dynamics are at play.

In difficult interactions, often the person with the power is the most relaxed, even when he or she is using strong language. When, for some reason, the outcome of a conversation doesn't really matter to us, when it is unlikely to affect us personally, the exchange is nothing more than a game – a sparring match. Even so, above all else, it's a match that we want to win. We have to be right because our egos demand it. We all like to have the final say, particularly when it emphasizes that we don't have to change.

Tough conversations

When a manager goes into a tough meeting with a subordinate, no matter what is exchanged – even if there were to be a little compromise – the manager usually has the last word. There may not be much tension during such a conversation, even when one or other participant has to hear some unpleasant things. The dynamics might play out differently, and not all managers hold the power, even from their position of privilege. There could be other factors involved. For example, the subordinate may go into the meeting with little power but a high degree of confidence, expecting that a hoped-for pay increase will be forthcoming. Those sorts of conversations result in either a big victory or a big defeat rather than anything in between.

Our blessed kinks result in many of us opining in haste and repenting at leisure. When we do have opinions, we rush to share them, only to realize later that the confidence we had was based on nothing more solid than our own thoughts. Sometimes, I'll happily write on social media about politicians or famous people. But if the subjects of my tweets were in the room with me, would I want them to read what I'd written? There is something about the relative anonymity of being behind a screen that emboldens us. The feeling seems to be similar to that of having a pack mentality – the belief that there is safety in numbers. So the dynamic of who has power changes online.

What occurs on social media is the result of human behaviour, rather than the sole fault of the platforms. Social media are a blank canvas on which we have painted a garish nightmare. And when we believe that we have nothing to do with the nightmare, we are fooling ourselves because we're all involved. For example, we might respond to an unkind tweet by saying something unkind ourselves. I have seen responses, calling out deplorable opinions and attitudes, that can sometimes rival the original 'crime' for sheer nastiness; those who write such responses are blind to their own awfulness. Whatever we bring to the platform – good or bad – will go on display there.

When we truly consider our own behaviour in these spaces, we are more likely to have a moderate approach to an argument, which would give us a greater chance of teasing out the truth.

Not enough time

The time it would take to understand each person's unique contribution to the world would be huge. It is a commitment that many of us don't believe we have the room to undertake. Instead, to sort out the world and make decisions quickly, we use stereotypes. We see someone; we put him or her into a box, and the box guides us in our treatment of that individual.

The question 'What do you do?' helps us to identify who another is in relation to us; whether the person is of a higher, lower or similar status. It might help us to decide how to relate to him or her. I have to admit that I'm guilty of pigeonholing people based on what they do for a living. Of course, the reality is that people are much more complex than what they do or which family they come from, even if they say about themselves, 'What you see is what you get.'

But how can we see? When you first meet me, you couldn't possibly know all those details I shared earlier about my upbringing. How could you know about all the joys, pains and everything in between that have helped to shape who I am? How could you have any idea about what will upset me because of buried pain or delight me because of a pleasant memory?

To see progress, we first have to remember that everyone else is *other*. No two people see everything in exactly the same way. When we communicate, we should start with this foundational level of under-standing or, more pertinently, misunderstanding. There is no singular story for anything, no matter how black and white we think something is. What do two different people mean when they say that they want to end inequality? What disparate individuals believe to be inequality, the causes of inequality and the solutions to inequality will vary.

The pain of difference might seem insurmountable during a tough conversation, particularly because of the misunderstandings, tensions and blind spots that will inevitably be present. To understand and embrace difference as a starting point can help to take the sting out of disagreement, which will be there whether we want to acknowledge it or not. If we were to try to listen to understand first, to be open to persuasion and to persuade rather than dominate, we would probably be more relaxed on entering the necessary dialogues for change. Such an attitude would signal that we were ready to look for solutions.

The two-way street of misjudgement

If we think that the world could be better, we are correct in that assumption. However, we must also accept that there is no single, quick way of getting there; there are no silver bullets. For a start, we aren't privy to every other person's experience, so our points of view are inevitably skewed. We make misjudgements all the time and mischaracterize others, just as they do us. For solutions to be found, our communications require fluidity, as well as boundaries; they have to be honest and respectful concerning other people's truth – elements that should flow both ways, especially when a relationship has to be built from scratch.

We don't have to accept that everything someone says as the truth; neither should we believe that everything they argue for is a lie. We can occupy the middle ground. When we move away from the fringes, we move away from the deep trenches of our opinions. Much of the time, we seem to commit everything to remaining in those trenches, becoming bogged down with our ideals and dislike of others with whom we disagree. We prefer hunkering down to ruthlessly examining and possibly giving up the beliefs in which we've invested so much. A fairer world won't spring out of blind loyalty to our convictions; it will arise from our releasing some of the views that we hold most dear, particularly when they don't serve the greater good. For these reasons, I find it difficult to align myself politically. The right can be rigid in its views; it receives a hard time for that. The left can seem very idealistic; it gets a hard time for that. Often, it is the centre in which elections seem to be won and progress is made.

I feel paralysed when I think about writing on these subjects. There are so many nuances and only so many words. Is it possible to distil my entire philosophy into one unpopular idea? Will I be misunderstood because I don't mention a particular group or issue?

There will be many who disagree with me, which is all right. I'm passionate about the change I want to see, and I think we have yet to explore some ways which could help the world to reach that goal. Sometimes, we have to be willing to be misunderstood. After all, road to change often begins with a little chaos – with lots of misunderstanding before communication improves, allowing us to keep talking, acting and moving forwards.

What can we already see?

It is easy to recognize obvious blind spots possessed by others: those of organizations or groups of people. We must be humble and gracious enough to see blind spots in ourselves, and to recognize how the different contributions we all have to offer make up the larger whole. We must also acknowledge when collective attitudes or inertia are holding progress back. We have to care enough about injustice to be honest about who we are and where we are, rather than where we think we should be. True progress cannot begin from a point that doesn't exist or from a position nobody holds. When there is blindness, we should take care that it isn't wilful. We should accept people as they are, with all their flaws and positive attributes, without making instant, negative judgements about them. After all, wouldn't we want others to give us the benefit of the doubt, particularly when they don't know us?

We all need to see the common threads that bind us together, no matter how divorced we may be from certain details; a big-picture vision of equality can help us to reach an understanding. Common ground must be coveted and sought after, even when we don't agree on every single detail.

The theory of self-worth

Someone once asked me what one thing I would change about the world if I could. My response was that I'd like everyone to know their worth.

Various social injustices have persisted for so long that they have distorted the way we see ourselves and one another. They have opened a gap that has never been closed. Some, who are very privileged, feel undeserving of all that they have, so they don't feel whole. Such feelings can affect how they see and treat themselves and, ultimately, how they relate to others. Some, who have been deprived of opportunities because of an accident of birth, see a world that tells them they are undeserving. And, without wise support, they come to believe this lie.

A sense of unfairness is deeply felt on all sides for a variety of reasons. And, of course, it's neither possible nor fair to make direct comparisons about how various issues affect different people, particularly when those problems remain unexpressed. Just because we don't or can't articulate what something is or what it means to us, doesn't mean the associated feelings don't exist. If anything, the damage to our emotional health is greater when we are unable to express what troubles us. When we feel deep shame about who we are or what we do, we are less able to accept others as they are; instead, we punish them harshly for the way we feel. When we can express what we think and feel, and are able to embrace fully our humanity, we can begin to take steps towards embracing others, and begin to explore honestly how to find the solutions we all want.

Most humans feel insecure about some part of themselves. Those who are very insecure will always try to bring others down. If there are few limits to how negatively we feel about ourselves, there will be few limits to the ways in which we lash out. Delineating the reasons for this would require another book entirely, but what I do know is that self-acceptance allows us to be proud of who we are, honest around what has to change and leaves room for us to celebrate other people, cultures and ideas. If more of us were to inhabit this space most of the time, celebrating our own cultures wouldn't mean having to snub those different from ours, and being passionate about our own ideas wouldn't mean having to squash or dismiss the beliefs of others. Feeling good about who we are never has to mean denigrating or degrading anyone else. If our individual and collective internal resilience were to grow and we were able to use words in their correct context, instead of misusing them, the result would be more effective discourses.

For example, we could begin discussions by checking whether both sides define 'racism' similarly. Often, when someone calls a Black person racist, he or she is using the dictionary definition. What one person defines as 'racist', others might say is 'prejudiced',[2] especially those people of colour who view racism as more structural and systemic, involving dominant White power structures. From this position, a person from a minority group can't be racist; rather, he or she might be prejudiced. If we were to develop this argument, how would 'racist' be defined in a situation involving Asians and Black people, without dominant White involvement? What is the correct term when an offence arises in a Black space where White people are the abused minority?

If we want to have these conversations – and we should – we have to be on the same page before the exchange begins. We have to agree on what certain, emotive words mean in the context of a specific conversation. Also, to begin from a place mutual understanding, we have to set aside our need to be right.

Word duality

There must be both individual and collective commitment to understanding. Although not explicitly expressed, there has, ironically, been a commitment to misunderstanding for a long time.

Terms such as 'race card', 'privilege' and 'oppression' are bandied about before we even try to understand what the other is saying; conversations that might have been profitable shut down quickly; hollow debate arises instead. Such discourse originates in our blind spots, and when there are too many of these exchanges, it becomes hard to dismiss them as one-offs. Rather, they become the norm; our defensiveness around them grows and so do our blind spots. We become fragile and shut down at the mention of certain words and, as a result, shut out whole groups of people who are bringing their social-justice issues to the table. To try to ameliorate such reactions in ourselves, we should be aware of when we want to roll our eyes, stop listening and harden our hearts.

To be less defensive requires us to be more accepting of new ideas and ways of seeing. If the world were fairer, we would want to receive new ideas. Even if we weren't able to agree with or accept them, the very act of being open to hearing about the unfamiliar would change everything about our dialogue. We shouldn't enter a conversation when we don't think we can be wrong; we won't converse – we'll just argue.

We all have opinions of which we are certain; those that are informed by our faith, our upbringing and our experiences. Sometimes, however, we have to suspend our disbelief to hear someone else clearly. It's fine to listen and say, 'I hear you and I respect that, but I don't agree', while hoping that the other person respects us for opening our ears and heart, despite our different perspective. Giving others some slack makes understanding and compromise far more likely than entering into a conversation with a closed mind. Of course, it is easier to say that we want to understand a different point of view and harder to do. But to be truly committed to finding solutions by improving the ways in which we understand others, we must carry our intentions through. Are those of us on the side of the majority – who believe the few who think differently are deplorable – willing to open our ears and hearts to the few? Are we prepared to try to understand them and their perspectives?

To help me think through my arguments before entering interactions about social-justice issues, I try to imagine how another person might react if I were to behave in a certain way. If I were to have a partner or friend who said, 'You have wronged me. I want you to apologize only as I see fit. I will set the terms because you're wrong', how long would such a relationship last? It would break down because an apology would be valid only if it were given in a certain way. The relationship would be draining and I'd avoid the other person. If, in a discourse about social justice, the person who has the power or the dominance were to say, 'I will help you but only in my way; by my rules. You must do exactly as I say', there would inevitably be a breakdown in negotiations. We can't possibly know or comprehend all the factors that have shaped the other person's views, but we can be open to trying to understand each other, and to think through together the best course for reaching a mutually beneficial solution.

What does your best look like?

The good news is that most of us know how to be our best. Most of us can be fair and compassionate. We are capable of giving others a second chance. We understand what it is to do the right thing, even when there is pressure not to do so. We know how to protect people and fight their corners. All we need is to extend that graciousness to *everyone*: those to whom we naturally would and those to whom we naturally wouldn't. We should be alert for double standards, especially in ourselves, and recognize that all the questionable stuff isn't just done or said by *other* people. The good, bad, ugly and everything in between also reside inside us. We must challenge the compulsion only to accept or believe those in our group: the people who look, think and behave as we do. We must acknowledge that our blind spots hinder progress. We must make the effort to acquire a well-rounded view of the world so that we can work out how to be part of the solution.

7

A singular narrative

You are traffic

I've never met anyone who sits in a traffic jam and thinks, 'I'm holding up all the people behind me. I am traffic, and I'm sorry about that.'

We are traffic, although we tend to think we aren't; rather, we believe that all the others around us are the traffic holding us up. Our blind spot means that we don't see ourselves as part of the problem – we merely sit in traffic; we are not traffic. The trouble is that everyone else is thinking the same thing: that everyone else is the problem rather than them. We have a singular narrative that says we are OK but you aren't. If you were like us, the world would be a glorious, traffic-free place. But we are all holding people up; we are all everyone else's problem.

By complaining that we're stuck in traffic, we give away our power and our ability to take an active role. We believe that we are being victimized by people and factors beyond our control. We are not wrong that other people are traffic; it's the fact that we exclude our own role as traffic that makes the story untrue. Saying that we aren't protagonists doesn't fit the tale. It's a narrative told purely from a single point of view – ours – without considering how we are inconveniencing others.

We tell this kind of singular narrative in many ways, about many things, which usually absolves us from having to take action, particularly with regard to social-justice issues. We tell ourselves it's not our fault; we are bystanders who are helpless to make a difference. It's why, despite knowing that racism and sexism exist, we don't seem to know anyone who admits to being either racist or sexist. But, of course, we might be able to identify a person who is a bigot, provided he or she is several degrees removed from us or from an older generation. It's why we're slow to identify racism as the reason that Black mothers are five times more likely to die in childbirth. We prefer not to think of racism as the major

87

factor because, although we understand that it exists and the statistics are true, we don't want to relate either to that nice midwife we know. We prefer not to know whether, as we sit in traffic, we are complicit in creating traffic and benefiting at the expense of everyone behind us. After all, we're just trying to reach our destination.

Yet we are all more than onlookers. We are the protagonists in society's story. Which roles do we really play?

Our singular story

There is a singular story we tell about ourselves, and nearly everybody has a similar three-stage version.

1 We make a caveat: 'I'm not perfect. I've made my share of mistakes.'
2 We absolve ourselves of mistakes: 'Overall, I am good. I have good intentions. I love most people, most of the time.'
3 We prematurely beatify ourselves: 'I hope to leave a good legacy.'

Most of us can admit that there is probably a gap between the story version of ourselves and who we really are. We all want others to see us at our best, yet we are all complex. We have many facets, including not so pleasant ones and everything in between. But this streamlined version of events is the overarching narrative that we tell. The gap between the publicized self and the real one is something that we don't want other people to notice. If they do notice, we don't want them to say so.

Occasionally, we meet those who don't believe that they are good, but they are few and far between. Even those who acknowledge their unreasonableness will still give a caveat for their behaviour. Such a caveat involves circumstances beyond their control or childhood problems. As a whole, we all tend to shy away from taking personal responsibility – after all, we're not traffic.

The gap between who we are and who we want other people to think we are is replicated at the larger societal scale, which is why people say things such as, 'I'm so embarrassed by our president/prime minister/ government.' When we haven't voted for a government, we quickly distance ourselves from its dodgy decisions. Yet the thought that we might be judged by association bothers us. We believe a government's questionable performance reflects poorly on us as individuals. We fall victim to our own stereotyping. After putting others in a box, we can't help but do the same thing to ourselves.

Most people personalize things: we see a car accident and think, 'I was passing that spot just yesterday. It could have been me.' Possibly, but it wasn't. We can't help doing so; it's very human. It's why it's hard, when we discuss injustice, not to think of ourselves as we scrabble around for a frame of reference to encourage ourselves and others to care.

Mind the gap

The personalization of this gap is replicated by most groups. For example, a White person might say, 'I can't believe that our country is so racist. I'm ashamed to be White'; alternatively, a Black person might say, 'Look at what those Black people are doing. It's so embarrassing'. We, or anyone we know, might not be doing the racist or embarrassing thing, but we still feel uncomfortable when we witness it. The greatest discomfort occurs when we see a behaviour (of which we ourselves are not guilty) that is often stereotypically assigned to our own culture. Because we share characteristics with the perpetrators, we may be ashamed to be associated with what they do or say, and we are more likely to notice the behaviours when they occur. Also, we suspect the behaviours are proving the stereotypes and that, as members of the wider group, we will somehow be judged by association. These reactions stem from the fact that we are always judging others (because we all hold many biases) and that we believe others are always judging us. So, whether or not the observed behaviour has a direct impact on us, it rankles.

Most of us have almost certainly used phrases that begin thus:

'Black people are so . . .'
'White people are like . . .'
'Women are so . . .'
'Men are just . . .'

The impulse to make sweeping generalizations is buried deep in us. Blanket statements about a group are usually made when none of its members is present. Despite our speaking about others in such a way, we are offended when they do something similar.

We use such labels because they are easy; we don't believe them to be personal (in our minds). It's just our way of easily fitting other people into boxes. In that way, we can work out how to relate to them. Sadly, shorthand of this kind becomes truth, which is why singular narratives are unhelpful. Over time, our minds become conditioned by this language to the extent that misogyny, for example, doesn't exist only in men. Anyone can internalize misogynistic thinking and anyone can act out misogynistic behaviour.

When we apply labels and singular narratives to whole groups of people, it shines a light on us and our thinking. It exposes how many gaps there are between our perception and reality. Not many of us would accept that stereotypes about our common cultural characteristics are true – precisely because they're not. It stands to reason, therefore, that the narratives we have for others aren't true either.

We are not our jobs

We use our singular story to place ourselves in the world. Just as stereotypes do, singular stories help us to understand our position in relation to other people. We tell the stories so often that we become attached to them, even when we know they're not true. We guard them from anyone and anything that could potentially undo our construction.

Someone from a working-class background once told me that it's mostly middle-class people who ask others, when they first meet, what they do. I hadn't noticed that before, but then I started noticing it all the time. On the one hand, it's a perfectly valid question to ask when first meeting someone; on the other, it's a yardstick. Years ago, when I told others that I was a newsreader, they would visibly warm up to me and become more interested; they would smile and be more open. For all I knew, they were thinking: 'She's important. She's on the telly. We know someone on the telly!' Of course, I sometimes also saw surprise:

there aren't many Black female newsreaders. The conversation would sometimes continue like this:

'How did you get into that, then?'

'I have a Master's in Broadcast Journalism.'

Cue more warmth and more smiling; I can see the cogs turning: 'She's done it the proper way; without "help" from a diversity scheme.'

I'm loath to call this bad behaviour. Such thinking probably stems merely from ignorance.

Stories about ourselves and others help us to piece together a jigsaw, and the process of fitting the pieces helps us to make sense of the bigger picture. Clarity is what we seek to solidify an understanding of the world that proves us right and our thinking correct. We especially want to understand where people whom we don't know, or have just met, fit.

These days, when I meet someone, I make the effort to ask questions other than those about work. It's hard because I'm so conditioned to find out what people do, as if it defines who they are. Many people define themselves by their jobs, their class, where they live and those with whom they associate. When we can see something clearly and communicate it well, it feels neat and tidy. We stereotype ourselves just as much as we do others.

The exit

When Brexit happened, some people put the working-class vote down to a lack of knowledge and education. I don't think it was that simple. There were probably a number of reasons why the working classes voted as they did:

- they believed a singular narrative about the world around them;
- they shared a growing unhappiness with the perceived changes in our culture;
- they believed that they were being displaced by other groups;
- they felt overlooked and that their collective importance had diminished;
- they believed that no one cared about what they thought or felt.

Whether or not we agree with what people want to say, there are definitely new social rules about the things we can no longer say out loud. I'm not going to call it political correctness, which is too basic a term and doesn't mean what I'm trying to articulate. But many people feel gagged. I am a big believer in free speech. I think there are many things that do need to be said which we can't and, of course, there are also many good reasons why certain things shouldn't be said. This issue of free speech is complex, and I understand why some people feel aggrieved about being silenced in certain ways. For many – with regard to the issues brought up by Brexit – the only place where they could truly express their frustration, and say what they wanted to say, was in the voting booth.

Many cultural and social-justice revolutions start with closed conversations. The limited group of people having the discussions tend to be more passionate about the issues that matter to them and so have an increased determination to find solutions. Let me stop there; this is a singular narrative that I've begun to spin. It's very easy to refer to things anecdotally, to fill in the blanks and to reach a conclusion that seems plausible enough, thanks to my blind spot. How would I know that the members of small groups are passionate and more likely to find solutions? Even if it were true of some, it couldn't be true of all.

We do this sort of thing all the time. Any narrative can take root and become real for us, with a bit of truth. However, a simplistic view of why some people voted the way they did in the Brexit referendum is as likely to be true as it is to be untrue, which is why we must thoroughly check whatever we believe to be true. We have to ask more questions to prevent anecdotal evidence, backed up with few facts and not much data, from becoming truth. Injustice feeds off assumptions to survive. It is only when a fuller picture of a situation is revealed, with the aid of others (our 'car mirrors'), that we are likely to have a clearer view of the solutions.

Who is 'us'?

The power of the stories that we tell ourselves prevent us from seeking out those who are different so that we may feel comfortable, safe and affirmed. We don't often examine why we think the way we do. For example, there are those who might say, 'People like us are being pushed out of our way of life.' When asked to explain, their response is often vague; either they can't pin down what they think is happening or they don't want to.

Because we're reasonable and good people, when we hear that something is happening, we assume that it probably is, even when there is little or no evidence. We can easily defend our shortcomings and persecute others for theirs. We don't want things to change; we don't want the challenge or the complexity. The status quo and our stories work for us. We don't want to rock the boat and lose whatever it is that we have. And, anyway, are things *really* that bad? We will never be hungry for justice as long as we are full of privilege.[1] The tendency not to want to change is linked to how comfortable we are. But who are 'we'? Who is 'us'?

We talk about *our* culture, the way *we* do things and *us* versus them. The tricky thing about the language of 'us and them' is that lines are drawn in sand rather than in anything concrete. The only person who is likely to be certain about whom he or she includes, when saying 'us', 'we' and 'ours', is the person talking. Even then, he or she might not actually be sure. So, when we refer to 'British people', do we actually mean 'White English people', 'White British people' (that is, Whites from all four UK nations), 'all those born in the UK' or 'all those who hold a British passport'?

People who blithely use the term 'British' can become quite flustered when pressed to define what they mean by the term. It might dawn on them that they are unsure of whom they are including. Few of us think deeply about such labels until asked to do so, and then we might not be sure how to articulate what we really mean. On occasion, individuals say to me, 'You lot' or 'Your lot', when referring to Black people. I know exactly what they mean but I ask them to clarify because I want to hear them say it. In some cases, they give the answer and quickly qualify it with 'But not you!' They back away from saying what they mean because it would expose what and how they truly think.

In the world of dating, people often ask, 'What's your type?' I have answered that question very differently depending on where I am and who is asking. The truth is, meeting someone face to face and identifying what attracts us is different from filling in a list on a dating site.

When it comes to using a dating app, we are making judgements and choices about things that would be hard or even impossible to know about someone, even if we were to meet them in the flesh. Would I date an atheist? Would I go out with someone over 6 feet 4 inches? Would I mind if he had children? There is a decreased chance of opposites attracting when selecting from a list. The choices we make may result from the way we feel that day or from basing them on past selections. If so, our choices stem from stereotyping, not chemistry. Picking a possible partner based on a criterion such as how much he or she earns is a risk; that number could go up or down within the year. It is a snapshot of who they are today, but not who they could be. Yet we use such indicators to work out if someone would make a suitable life partner. When we first meet someone in a social setting and say 'Hello', we don't usually analyse all this sort of information. However, when asked to start listing preferences, we may select criteria that aren't really all that important to us simply because we've been asked to do so.

A list based on values might be a better start. Even so, it would still be a crude measure. Just because, as potential partners, we both value kindness and honesty does not mean that we will get on. There are many factors that make us who we are. The essence of who we both are can't be found by highlighting certain characteristics and preferences; we are both much more complex. The best way to understand someone is to get to know them.

The them-and-us narrative is a very inefficient way of making sense of the world. For each of us, if we're honest, most other people fall into the 'them' category. I've met Black people who say they are unique because they don't have rhythm or they can't dance. How many Black people fit that description? *So* many, including me, with regard to dancing! But there is a narrative that Black people have rhythm and are good dancers. If a person of African heritage were to have neither rhythm nor the ability to dance, a non-Black person somewhere would be surprised, even shocked, and exclaim, 'But you're Black!' How many women are not emotional and/or maternal? Lots. The more individuals you know in a group, the more you realize that 'us' is fractured and disparate.

So is it possible to group 'us' broadly? If so, what are the criteria? I think it is possible to group people according to characteristics, provided we understand that, although individuals comprise groups, groups don't define individuals. It takes more than a single characteristic for us to be like one another. Individuals from various groups have to be willing to understand one another and to persevere with relationships, even when it's tricky to negotiate differences. Families, when they work well, are a great example of this. Communities founded on shared values tend to be as well. It is not guaranteed that individuals in a group defined simply by a single characteristic, such as gender, race, (dis) ability, sexuality or class, will live and breathe in harmony. There are more likely to be greater levels of agreement when a variety of groups of people intersect: the more intersection, the more agreement is likely, but it's not a given. A group of Black women who are able-bodied, straight and middle class will have different opinions and a variety of blind spots.

It is not that we should resist belonging to groups; rather, we should see them as fluid. We should do so not because our characteristics change but because, concerning different issues, we oscillate between being 'us' and being 'them'. The more that groupthink is required for acceptance in any group, the more niche the group becomes. While there is a feeling of safety in communicating only with people who are like us, doing so will never bring about a fairer world.

Can people change?

We have become so invested in protecting 'us' and what's 'ours' that we have become blind to the opportunities that might present themselves if 'us' were rather more inclusive. When our boundaries remain rigid, we prevent communication and connection with others. It is not only the kind of people we believe oppose change who exhibit this kind of rigidity; the people who want more inclusion often exclude those they don't see as progressive.

This attitude is not the best way to reach a solution. Our world will never be inclusive while we use exclusion as a tool of change. We can call this outlook cancel culture[2] but a more appropriate term for this type of exclusion might be 'rejection culture'. It is a culture in which people are considered beyond the pale because they disagree with a certain behaviour or philosophy; they are *personae non gratae*. For the safety of society, some individuals are locked away because they abuse others physically, mentally or emotionally. Are we going to lock people up and throw away the key simply because they disagree with us?

We have to ask ourselves whether we believe that people can change. Can their thoughts and attitudes change? If not, then why try to persuade anyone at all? 'Them' will never ever be 'us' if we have that point of view. If communicating to see change is what we seek, how can shutting down conversations help? Many of us dislike our views being questioned. We close down exchanges by calling those on the opposite side bigoted, racist or misogynistic. Conversely, the other side might say that we are playing the race card. This style of discourse counters understanding. Unless those who believe differently from us are allowed to speak, we won't know what they think. When we have an idea what they think and what motivates them, better awareness and increased understanding will be the foundation from which to push for justice for all.

Intent and impact matter in this space; sometimes the impact of what is said can be painful even when the intent was not to hurt. Nevertheless, if the wider discourse is hindered from progressing because of one emotive point, and if there's nothing a person can do to be accepted by the other side, why bother to engage? We are caught in a cycle of misunderstanding; our conversations lack openness and honesty; and there are penalties for not agreeing on everything with everyone. This stalemate is a catastrophe for seeking justice.

To use the analogy of a dating app again, it's as if you were missing out on a relationship with an amazing guy because you ticked a particular box that causes him to be excluded from a choice of suitable partners. Rejecting him for being an inch too short means that you're rejecting the bigger truth of who he is. In a similar way, we are rejecting solutions because we don't like the packaging. The pull of justice has to be stronger than that. In seeking boundaries rather than walls, we don't have to sacrifice ourselves or our dignity. Instead, we have to become open to telling new stories about people who are not like us. And, while we find out more, it is very important that we listen, truly listen, and choose not to take offence.

Group as we'd like to be grouped

We can sometimes fall into the traps of thinking that that all men are misogynistic or all White people are racist, and of grouping people in a way that we ourselves wouldn't want to be grouped. Can we truly desire equality while declaring that White, middle-class men are evil and the scum of the earth? (I'm not pandering to White sensibilities; I certainly wouldn't accept being grouped in such a generalized way.) Are some White, male middle-class men problematic? Yes. But some are great champions of inclusion and they do the work. Are some middle-class Black women problematic? Yes. However, we are not all aggressive and angry. Every group includes individuals who behave in ways that others wouldn't and who believe things others don't. In every one of them, there are people who share more with us than we know. We should resist grouping others, and writing them off, based on certain shared characteristics or views.

Every singular story about ourselves is founded on the belief that all we are and do is reasonable; we justify our thoughts and behaviour because, as far as we're concerned, our intent is usually good. Deep down, however, we know it's not entirely true. For us to be right, when it comes to people with whom we disagree, not only do we say they are wrong but we also say that their motives are impure and their intentions are unreasonable. Even when those on the other side of the debate say things we want to hear, we don't trust them. Every single one of us must reject the uninformed narratives that we impulsively adopt. We can choose to be reasonable, measured and informed or unreasonable, irrational and ignorant. We must not pretend that good resides only in us. If we were to stop pretending that we alone are the heroes, we wouldn't be able to hide in the gap between the way we see ourselves and the way we want others to see us.

The intersection of injustice

'Us and them' is a complicated and ever-moving picture. Sometimes 'us' means women: some of the injustices we face come from men of all races, including our own. Sometimes 'us' means other people of the same race and, possibly, heritage. Sometimes 'us' means those who belong to the same class. Then again, 'us' might be something else entirely and may sit at an intersection of many characteristics. The more intersections, the fewer there are of 'us' and the more there are of 'them'. For example, if we were to define an ethnic group by adding an increasing number of other factors to race, such as gender, class, sexuality, disability, home ownership, employment status and so on, the smaller the group concerned would become.

We change the meanings of words to suit our arguments. We choose not to see the flaws in ourselves; rather, we defend them, even when we have to reject the truth to do so. We are, at times, knowledgeably ignorant and we don't want to change – all to preserve our singular stories. We don't want to face the fact that we ourselves have internalized the sexist, racist, classist and superior attitudes that we deplore. We don't want to face the fact that being categorized as 'oppressed' doesn't stop us from exhibiting similar behaviours to those of the 'oppressors'. Even when we try to be fair, we find ourselves excluding and dismissing whole groups of people. We remain rigid. We console ourselves by repeating our stories and saying that 'it's just the way it is'. Unconscious bias becomes conscious when we refuse to fill in the blanks and learn, especially about the various ways in which intersectionality highlights our differences and similarities. People of a variety of ethnicities might be more closely bound by class and gender than by race. Yet it seems that one characteristic must trump all the others, despite our being the sum of a number of characteristics and more.

Humans have always craved safety in numbers; so, surely, the best way to be truly safe is to be as open and welcoming to as many people as possible. Sadly, though, the evidence shows that this narrative is not what we experience. We know about this more inclusive way of being, but many of us choose to let our biases and prejudices go unchecked, and so we are more divided than ever.

Unravelling world views

Affirmation versus challenge

When we see the world a certain way, we seek out others who think as we do. This process is easiest with people who are already much like us.

When we meet someone new, we indulge in exchanges that help us to discover what we share:

'I played netball at school.'

'Me, too!'

'I hated my twenties!'

'Me, too! We have so much in common!'

Being around those who think the way we think and live the way we live affirms what we believe about ourselves; it's comforting. As we grow in our knowledge of our new friends, we realize there is plenty that we do *not* have in common. Then it dawns on us that we are no longer being affirmed; we are being challenged. This change in the tenor of the relationship might cause new friends to reject each other.

This scenario has played out in my own life a number of times. It might have done so in yours too. Sometimes, we do need to put distance between ourselves and others because there are very good reasons for doing so. Some people are harmful to be around. Alternatively, it might be that there are personality clashes or being in the other person's company is like looking into a mirror and disliking what we see. Whatever the reason, it's not possible to get on with or have relationships with every single person on earth.

As we grow older, our stories become more refined and the number of chapters increases. It becomes harder to change parts of the story, unless we are willing to lose our egos and expose the gap between the way we see ourselves and what we want others to see. We think that racism and sexism are simply a rejection of other people. I believe that they are symptoms of self-rejection that result in the bigoted individual projecting stereotypes on to and rejecting others. In an attempt to keep our personal stories intact, our stories about others have to be that way too. Often, when people fail to conform to the stereotypes that help us to categorize them, it can be too challenging for us because it indicates that our stories – our understanding – might be wrong.

Self-rejection and exclusion

When a company tries to implement an inclusive, anti-discriminatory employment policy, the response from some staff might be: 'We shouldn't hire people just because they are Black/female/disabled/gay. We should hire the best person for the job.' If we were to move beyond the fact that there are very probably people with any and all these characteristics who could do the job to a very high standard, why should their being hired bother those already established in the company? It disturbs those staff members because they have quiet, unexpressed fears about their place in the world. They're not sure whether they're enough or their chances of promotion will decrease because of the inclusive policy. It is inconceivable to some that they might have been hired precisely because they are White and/or male, and fit into the existing dynamic and culture of the workplace. Yet this has often been the case.

Affirmative action for White people is an enduring but unexpressed fact. We are aware of this unspoken policy but, because of the gap between who we are and who we want people to think we are, we say that the best person should get the job. Nevertheless, we choose someone with whom we're comfortable, but who might not have been the best person for the job. Also, there's the lurking discomfiting suspicion that we ourselves might have been recruited not because we were the best overall candidates but simply because we were the best identikit candidates – and that's a big difference.

What many people fear is the loss of automatic opportunity. The idea of sharing, and having to fight harder for, opportunities with a wider group can cause individuals who used to be shoo-ins for certain roles to say that the 'best people' must be chosen. They are personalizing the process, and relating it back to what it means for them and what it says about them. On the surface, they seem to be rejecting diversity. In reality, they are rejecting their need to examine how they reached their positions and what helped them to get there. They avoid considering that perhaps they have jobs from which others more capable were excluded because they didn't 'fit in' quite so well. They suspect that if the world were truly equal, they might not have opportunities to which they believe themselves entitled. For those who think that White people and/or men are superior, the fact that other people are as good as, if not better than, they are (but didn't have the chance to prove it) seriously undermines their belief system.

What we see at the surface isn't always the truth. Superficial communication often hides something else. Rather than be offended by the assumptions made by people with a superiority complex, we should understand that their complex is very much their burden to carry and work through. They each have a story; they've found out their stories aren't true, so their world views unravel. Exposing what an individual truly thinks and feels is very challenging; it can bring out the worst.

Truly humbled

The progress we want to see will happen only when we are all willing to part ways with the stories about who we think we are. We all have work to do.

I remember vividly when I was a new presenter at BBC Midlands. I was young and very proud of myself and my achievement. Within a year, I had progressed quickly from online journalism to being on air, in front of a camera. I had not long left university, so I was doing well. From the age of 19 until then, I had been going through a difficult period, so my success at the BBC felt like a massive vindication. At the time, I thought I was very humble (and, at times, I was). However, one of my least humble moments was when I told someone what a good person I was because, unlike others in the newsroom, I spoke to everyone in the building – including the cleaners! How embarrassing: in my moment of 'humility', I exposed my unconscious thinking. The truth is that I thought I was special: I thought I was better than the cleaners. While verbally expressing my love for equality, I was also subconsciously expressing where I thought I was in the BBC's hierarchy.

We mustn't excuse poor behaviour but we should try to understand it, where it comes from and what we can learn. There's a saying that you should look down on others only when you help them. But we shouldn't look down on anyone at all. We are all confused without even knowing it. It is so easy for each of us to be patronizing or discriminatory. If the cleaners had heard what I'd said, they would have judged me instantly to be unpleasant and condescending, regardless of my warmth and friendliness towards them. Despite my not meaning the comment the way it sounded, it might have caused upset and offence. Sadly, there isn't always the chance to qualify what we mean and to allow others to understand that a comment said far more about us than about them. No matter the intent, the impact can be harmful, which is why we must use the tool of communication as well as we can. I don't want to condone poor behaviour, but if we were to put it into context and think carefully about the intention behind it, we might understand its origins a little better.

Many of us feel badly about ourselves owing to the words and actions of others, which we absorb and may come to believe as the truth. Someone else's inability to see our full humanity, with all its nuances and complexity, doesn't diminish that humanity. When something someone says or does is hurtful, we could take a moment to put ourselves in the other person's place and think about the reasons for his or her actions. When we are the ones on the receiving end of an ill-judged comment, it is a struggle to walk away from the narrative that has been imposed on us. The hope is that we can see when the impact isn't related to the intent, and we recognize when the impact has been harmful, despite the intent.

When the impact of a statement is aligned with the intent, and a person meant what he or she said, then we must understand that the individual's story is an issue for him or her to work through. There are many harmful stereotypes about Black women (and every other minority group). If I were to absorb all those narratives, I wouldn't be able to like myself.

Don't hate the label more than the injustice

People tend to hate being called 'racist' more than they hate being racist. Most react very strongly when accused of bigotry and vehemently deny it. If they are racist or sexist but are in denial about their true attitudes, it's because they haven't recognized the gap between their beliefs about themselves and the reality. Either they are not willing to accept that they are bigoted or, sadly, they think that their views are acceptable.

When confronting such people, it's important, first, to understand what we're dealing with. Second, we must realize that, even when people know they are bigots or recognize the existence of a gap, they don't want others to see them as such and they probably don't plan to correct their behaviour.

We don't usually know with whom we're dealing until we call something out. Hiding behind ambiguity in these situations is often preferable for those of us who don't want a tense exchange, even when we think we're right. Nevertheless, we can't escape the fact that, even when we paper over the cracks in our carefully constructed stories, our words and actions often give us away. In my own case, I obviously didn't see the cleaners as equals; I believed that I was doing something good – even exceptional – just by speaking to them. There is a passage from the Bible that highlights an important truth about what we say:

> A good man brings good things out of the good stored up in his heart, and an evil man brings evil things out of the evil stored up in his heart. For the mouth speaks what the heart is full of.
> (Luke 6.45)

In unguarded moments, who do you think you are? Have you always treated Black people as you do everyone else? How have you related to people with disabilities or to women? Why is saying that you treat others equally such a badge of honour for you? Might the reason be that, when you treat someone who is different well, you think you're going above and beyond the call of duty because – *really* – you don't believe that everyone *is* equal?

Sometimes, when we treat someone who is different fairly, we consider that treatment a kindness. Why? We don't usually have to point out that we are kind to our siblings, unless there is some underlying reason for there to be unkindness. We usually highlight the things to which we want to draw people's attention because we think it shows us in a good light.

At the times when I've been alerted to one of my own gaps, I've hidden in it and defended my position. Hiding in the gap means that I don't have to look at it or to understand and embrace who I truly am. Defending my position also means that I don't have to address it. Acknowledging the gap will show me that I'm too complex for comfort; it's much better to assume that I'm a straightforwardly nice person.

When we are responsible for a negative impact that results from bad intent, we don't want to admit it. We hate the label more than we hate what we've done. We might be embarrassed but we won't change because it means we have to admit that there was something wrong in the first place. The intent might not be evil, as such, but it is bad enough to harm someone else's prospects. For instance, those of us who are ambitious might have pushed aside or trampled on others to get ahead. We might have used their otherness to defend and justify our actions. If so, we would be guilty of perpetuating a singular story concerning stereotypes to protect our erroneous view of ourselves. Injustice exists in this world only because we exclude others for our own gain. Sometimes, what we want isn't necessarily wrong. For example, we may choose to fight for women's rights but ignore the plight of those with disabilities. Because we prefer to stand shoulder to shoulder with people who share our passion, we justify our choice to exclude others. If we want a just world, we must include everyone.

Injustice infighting

We all desire reductive narratives to help us to understand the world quickly, which is why we define and reduce whole cultures and people to stereotypes.

In the wake of George Floyd's death, a brief look at social media revealed many commentators claiming to know all the myriad things Black people were thinking and feeling. Each 'pundit' would, with lots of passion, say that all Black people were tired, angry, victims, had had enough and so on. From a quick survey of my Black friends, I discovered some felt that way and some did not. A number of commentators also assumed that those of us who were Black wouldn't want to talk about what had occurred in Minnesota and advised others not to message us. For my part, I didn't feel like that at all.

A huge blind spot is the assumption that everyone else thinks and feels as we do. On a social-media platform, when we receive a lot of 'likes' from people who agree with us, we accept them as confirmation that we are right to speak for others. But the reality is that we surround ourselves with people to whom we are similar and with whom we resonate; we follow people who say things with which we agree. This anecdotal evidence that seems to prove we're right is far from the whole picture. In a world inhabited by more than 7 billion people, even a million likes don't come close to a consensus. While we may choose to believe that any group we belong to is not monolithic, we are quick to point the finger at those who disagree with us – including those who are part of our group, whom we may even label traitors to the cause. This behaviour can also be found in splinter groups that have broken away to indulge in 'free-thinking': the members can begin to round on and cast out those who disagree with certain beliefs.

It's a tricky and complicated question: can we have a society that is fully inclusive when we exclude different (rather than harmful) views? This question is even more vexed when those similar to us disagree strongly with us. In the UK, many people see Black Conservatives as individuals who either don't think or are blind; they view them as turkeys who vote for Christmas. It's hard for some to accept that they just choose to think differently. Feminism is well known for these kinds of assumptions too. Feminists can be anything they want to be, except for housewives or lovers of fashion. I see similar examples of exclusion on many sides of many debates. We are wedded to our groups and our stories about who belongs inside, and we are anchored to the narratives that dictate how insiders should think and behave.

In our own worlds, we can set the rules. We cannot, though, unilaterally decide who is in and out on a wider scale. We should allow people to be themselves, even though it can make life messy. We should move away from demanding that we must all be in complete alignment before we can focus on much bigger goals. Obviously, when we disagree on too many points, then, perhaps, we should agree to disagree.

Admittedly, there are some people I've chosen to let go, not because they are bad but because our core values are very different. But, in general, I don't believe a condition of a friendship must be that we agree on everything. There's a maturity to valuing difference in those who are similar to us; there's respect in allowing them to express it. Progress is achieved when we stop the infighting – which is only ever a distraction – and choose to focus on all the things about which we do agree.

Are our memories true?

Our memories are not as good as we think they are. We often believe that we accurately remember the past and all its details. The memory may be clear to us but it is also clouded. A friend or relative might say, 'Do you remember such and such?' and we may reply, 'Oh, yeah! I'd forgotten about that.' The reasons for a certain detail being forgotten are very probably to do with singular narratives affecting the memory, no matter how good we might believe it to be.

Memories are filtered through our feelings and our emotions. When we recall things, we do so with bias – bias that keeps the constructed picture of ourselves intact. My two sisters and I remember events from our childhood very differently, sometimes wildly so. Over time, the way we remember incidents changes. Our understanding of the situations and their interpretation have altered; yet we continue to think our different versions of the memories are the accurate ones and, because there are three of us in my family, it means that one of us disagrees with the other two sometimes. This is why I have often struggled with the view that others' memories of how we might have once made them feel can be equated with what *actually* happened. It's not that I don't believe they remember feeling a certain way; I suspect that it's more to do with how they felt, and feel, about themselves. I'm not excusing unkindness or ill intent, which happens – sometimes very intentionally – but when we see ourselves in a mirror, we feel negatively about what we see. It doesn't matter how nice the person is showing us the reflection, we don't like it or, at that moment, the individual holding the mirror. The question is, are we willing to accept that someone else isn't necessarily the cause of our painful feelings? He or she might simply reflect what is already inside us.

We are all capable of taking part in interactions that result in bad memories for others. We all remember things the way we remember them – from our point of view. If we want to be fairer in conversations about memories, we must remove our biases before revisiting exchanges and events. We should prepare ourselves for the fact that we might be wrong; it's impossible to be right or the victim all the time. When we allow others to be imperfect or mistaken – human, in other words – we can be human too. We can reject the singular narratives that other people *are* the interaction we had with them because they aren't and neither are we.

We can invest so much in building the appearance of being good that we don't actually do good and become the 'good people' we want to be. All our focus is on ourselves and most of our energy is spent on the construction and maintenance of who we want people to think we are, which is a story that we can never live up to. While doing that work, we can't think about the needs of others.

So should we allow ourselves to be utterly exposed and vulnerable when taking part in a discourse?

I don't think so. We should accept that we can be with different people in a variety of ways; we can use different approaches and have different attitudes at various times. We should consider how best not to be hindered by an untrue story. Expending energy on building phoney images means that we avoid examining the past and the implications it has for the present. Incorporating other people's memories into our own would give us a fuller picture of our history and who we really are. With regard to doing so, the real challenge is the amount of humility required.

Shared history: different outcomes

This lack of accurate remembrance affects whole societies. A particular version of events told often enough will become the truth, basing not just the past but also the future on a false foundation – especially when a great many people say so. Can a multitude be wrong? Yes.

The death of George Floyd in the USA, in the summer of 2020, was filmed. A video showed a police officer kneeling on his neck for 8 minutes and 46 seconds. This video, sadly, was not the first to show a White police officer choking a Black man to death. Mr Floyd's death mobilized people across the planet. They marched and proclaimed on international stages that Black lives matter. In cities across the UK, there were anti-racism marches, despite the COVID-19 pandemic. These events go to the heart of how complex a story that involves so many people can be.

Commemorating evil? The statue of Edward Colston

There were many narratives in the aftermath of George Floyd's death; millions of memories were created during that time, specifically around people's awakening to or continuing the fight against anti-Black racism. In Bristol, during one of the protests, a statue was torn down and pushed into a river. All statues commemorate the past, usually in a celebratory way. This one was erected in 1895 and marked the life of Edward Colston, a merchant linked to the transatlantic slave trade. The statue itself and what happened to it were stark reminders of the historical inequality between Black people and White people and the different ways in which each group views history.

When we look at the UK's past, it's not just about British history or Black history or Asian history or whatever. And, although the outcomes have been unequal, these histories are not separate but must be considered to be interrelated. As Martin Luther King, Jr wrote:

> In a real sense all life is interrelated. All men are caught in an inescapable network of mutuality, tied in a single garment of destiny. Whatever affects one directly, affects all indirectly. I can never be what I ought to be until you are what you ought to be, and you can never be what you ought to be until I am what I ought to be . . . This is the interrelated structure of reality.[3]

The inequality of historical outcomes means that we all view our shared history through lenses of bias. Historical accounts can never be truly accurate because those who wrote them did so with bias. Even so, there are many different historians, and their various accounts together provide a range of perspectives that allow us to gain a fuller picture. How we, as individuals, see history will be depend on which side of it we sit. There were those who took advantage and those who were very badly treated (a massive understatement in some cases), and both sides passed on their legacies.

When the statue of the Bristolian merchant Edward Colston was torn down, it divided people greatly. To some, the statue was a monument to what it meant to be British. For them, Colston was a philanthropist, a benevolent man, who should be remembered as a father of the city. To others, he was a callous slave trader, who made his fortune from buying and selling human beings. During his time at the Royal African Company, he was involved in transporting 84,000 enslaved African men, women and children, 19,000 of whom died on voyages from West Africa to the Caribbean and the Americas. For many, the good he did in Bristol was ultimately rooted in evil and therefore irrevocably tainted, so his statue had to come down.

Here was a shared history, but the descendants of slave traders and the descendants of slaves held very different views about who this man was and what his legacy is. (I use these terms loosely; not all Black people are descendants of slaves and not all white people are the descendants of slave traders.) Also, on both sides, opinions were not solely based on personal history.

Was Colston a slave trader or a philanthropist? He was both. That truth is challenging for us. We want to categorize people as either good or bad, or kind or cruel, so that we know in which box they belong. We want to be able to pigeonhole others so that we have no tough decisions to make, and nothing complex with which to grapple. When we acknowledge that Colston was both a slave trader (responsible for the deaths of thousands) and a philanthropist (who used his profits to help his community), we can discuss whether one aspect is too horrendous to celebrate the other. But when both sides refuse to see the other point of view and refuse to see the whole picture, there can't be a productive conversation. I realize that this is a very emotional subject for some; this debate had been rumbling on for many years in Bristol.

As challenging as it is, we have to learn to remove some of the emotion from these conversations so that we can nail down the facts. It sounds cold, but have you ever been in a conversation with someone who was very emotional when you weren't? Perhaps you were the emotional one. Such exchanges are rarely productive; the differing emotional states hinder mutual understanding. Basically, we cannot begin a conversation from the point at which we would like those opposing us to be. We have to start where we all are – seeing things very differently at the outset.

There have been debates about other statues of people with complex pasts. Some have been taken down by local authorities. Given that, in the modern West, we have a shared understanding that slavery is evil, should such people be memorialized (which implies that they are exemplary and worthy of honour) and their statues allowed to remain? There are those who feel strongly that, despite the deaths and atrocities, the statues should stay.

In the end, protesters pulled down Colston's statue themselves, an action that resulted in much contention. The way the story was reported and debated was loaded with generalizations, when it needed nuance. The way the news agencies spun the facts is the way in which it is (and will be) remembered. What is incorporated and what is left out is important for our collective memories and future action. When we revisit the story of Colston's statue, we will use what was last said as our reference point. When that reference point is not accurate, an unequal outcome from a shared moment will once again breed division.

Lashings of bias

The whole Edward Colston statue incident was captured on video. We saw mostly, but not exclusively, White people with ropes, pulling it down and rolling it into the river. Yet the story in the press was about Black Lives Matter demonstrators and mobs tearing it down. If we were to hear this story after the fact, without video, we might conclude that the people removing the statue were Black.

This exemplifies the danger of singular narratives that do not give the full context. Without rounded explanations, we build lies. Social media and the press began to comment that Black people were taking down statues and wanted to remove the history of the country – 'our [White] history', even though it's a shared one. The Prime Minister, Boris Johnson, commented that history couldn't be Photoshopped by taking statues down; words such as 'woke' were thrown around; and the conversation became divisive. Of course, the Prime Minister missed the irony that the very action of selecting some people to be memorialized is a type of Photoshopping. There were many debates and myriad words were written about the battle for Britain's history and culture. The Colston statue story was told and repeated with no context, which meant fiction became fact. The nuanced reality was that there were both Black and White people opposed to its existence. Some might argue that the Black Lives Matter protests were actually a cover for removing the statue or that they provided an opportunity to take action regarding a long-standing issue. After all, not many people go to protests with ropes. Removing the statue was a desired outcome and the protests provided the momentum.

There were also marches in Oxford and London about other statues. Different people had different views about whether or not statues should come down and, if so, when, why and how but really, should we have even been talking about statues? Wasn't doing so a distraction from the original issues of inequality and murderous police brutality?

When it came to the aftermath of the killing of George Floyd, there were diverse and complex views among Black and White people but it was easier for many to see the narrative in two ways. The media version was not necessarily the true or fully informed one. Being unbiased is a standard for which many UK news outlets like to aim. Nevertheless, they often miss. We are only human, biases creep in, especially under the pressure of reporting a quick-moving story, when resources are few because of a global pandemic. The Bristol statue incident is not a one-off example of how our collective memories are made. Think of all the different ways that the stories we hear can be distorted. So many variables go into their presentation. How differently would we see the world if we were offered more complexity and nuance? We must remember that a country is not just it's history; it is also its present and future.

The Winterval that never was

In the winter of 1997–8, in my home town of Birmingham, there was a great deal of annoyance because Birmingham City Council planned to rename Christmas 'Winterval'. It was claimed that the change was made to avoid offending people of other faiths. It was outrageous! No one who wanted this change was either identified or quoted. It turned out that people of other faiths weren't the reason behind it; the whole idea was purely a marketing ploy. The name 'Winterval' was made up to promote all the activities the council were running from November to January, not just during Christmas. The council, of course, denied the story.

Denials are never allocated as much space as the original pieces, which take on a life of their own. In fact, the story returned for several years around Christmas; it even made national tabloid headlines in subsequent years but, despite the initial untruth, there was nothing to see.[4]

How much of our collective memory and the narratives we accept are based on nothing more than overactive imaginations at best and pot-stirring at worst? Despite many of these stories not having much substance or basis in reality, they are discussed at length at dining-room tables, at school gates and in pubs. So, no matter whether an apology is printed to retract or rectify the inaccuracy, the original, singular story sticks and causes much division. The residual impression is that people of other faiths want to cancel 'our British' Christmas. And Black people want to erase 'our' history.

A singular narrative, even when it has lots of detail, will eventually be distilled down to one idea. Memories based on inaccuracies stay at the back of people's minds. They don't encourage progress and greater cooperation; they don't encourage communication with people who are not like us or who may see things differently. The tension that people feel around these conversations means that, rather than thinking or concluding that we simply don't know all the facts, we avoid finding out more. We prefer, instead, to repeat what we've heard.

When those on all sides of the debate believe that their culture is being erased – even when it's not – great harm is done. It results in our thinking that everyone else wants to coerce and control us. People aren't necessarily fighting for statues to stay up; they are fighting because of what the removal of such commemorative pieces might mean for their own stories. Some White Britons believe that their pride in being British and in the UK's historical achievements is being undermined because of an imperial past that is categorized as evil. Just as many think that poor national government reflects badly on them personally, sectors of the British public believe that they are being associated personally with wicked aspects of the past.

Sometimes, we have to ask ourselves what, exactly, we are holding on to and why. We are all having separate conversations about the same issue. For those who wanted Colston's statue taken down, the discussion was in a very different space: if we celebrate a man who has done great harm, what are we saying to those whose ancestors were enslaved by him and others like him? And what are we saying about those who look like the slave traders? Does memorializing such a man imply that slavery doesn't matter? Does it say that it was evil but some good came out of it, so let's move on?

We are all affected by the long arm of history. Both sides ought to recognize that the intertwining histories which comprise our shared history cannot be unravelled. We have to accept that history must be told in its entirety, which it isn't presently. No one wants to Photoshop it; rather, we want a fuller telling of it. If that doesn't happen, nothing will change.

No one can claim British history as theirs alone. Our history must take everyone into consideration because it involves us all; it belongs to all of us, and all of us can learn from it to make better decisions in the present for everyone's best interest. Until we accept that fact, there will be no progress in our discussions.

Those involved in these national conversations are holding up a mirror, a rear-view one at that. Going over past ground is of little use beyond putting issues into context because we are so well acquainted with the problems already. We have been down these roads too many times not to contemplate trying a new approach. None of the sides participating in these debates has effectively communicated that they want to be understood, as opposed to just heard. What is it that we now need to say to move forwards?

8

Saviours

There are no more complicated power dynamics than those at play in the development sector, especially in relation to fighting poverty. The label 'White saviour' has become synonymous with international development. Terms such as 'poverty porn' are used to describe the images and narratives around raising funds for various causes. These phrases illustrate how complicated the relationships between the helpers and the helped have become over time and that, sometimes, the ends don't necessarily justify the means. Ethics and good clear judgement can become clouded as people try to do more to help and, increasingly, try to capture the public's attention to raise money.

To begin with, most charities are set up to help people rather than to make a profit. Once charities begin to grow, they need a greater number of staff, which requires more fundraising to pay the staff, as well as to provide for charitable needs. Staff salaries have to be paid before anyone receives aid because, without the staff, the charities' goals wouldn't be achieved. Growth and an ever-increasing emphasis on raising funds become locked in a vicious circle or feedback loop. Where the line should eventually be drawn is up for debate.

Donors think that they're funding vital charitable work, which they are, but they are also paying professional salaries, either directly or indirectly. A huge number of charities and NGOs want an increasing amount of our money to allow them to do more and more. So, like the news organizations in our fast-paced world, charities have had to resort to using clickbait to garner more funds, which means that they create increasingly provocative campaigns to grab attention. And when an organization does something at high speed, many other factors go unnoticed. For instance, has offensive wording been inadvertently used in the effort to attract attention? What does setting certain text next to certain images imply? Have the feelings of the case-study subjects been considered when producing the piece in which they are included?

The charity sector is very White and very middle class. Many of the staff believe that they are 'called' to this work, but only a few have an intimate knowledge of the people they are helping, who are usually thousands of miles away. Not all the employees can be sent on expensive trips abroad; it isn't a good use of money, despite the quandry this presents, that travelling to the regions concerned is one of the best ways to understand the issues.

Allyship[1] is best done relationally, which is what is lacking in much of the charitable sector. Employees do read the case studies and see the work of those on the front line. For most, however, the intimate knowledge required to do someone else's story justice just isn't there. I suspect that many of the subjects of the case studies would be surprised (or shocked) by how they are portrayed. They might be suffering and struggling but they would still consider themselves to be people who are fully human, living the rounded experience that encompasses love, loss and everything in between. To see themselves reduced to a poverty statistic and a photo or video would be humiliating and disappointing. We would have similar feelings if we were memorialized as hungry, poor and helpless. Charity workers can be deeply naive about what is truly happening: that is, that the complexities of a colonial legacy continue to fuel global poverty and inequality in the present. They also fail to be cognizant of the fact that, despite the charities' work to help a few people, inequality remains because the systemic power structures in the charities themselves and the countries in which they work are left unchanged.

Research shows that pictures of African children in poverty make the most income for charities. The visual narrative for many years has always been about people of colour – mostly Black people – being helped by almost exclusively White people. Many of these charities are usually run at a senior level by White people. Some might say that aid is provided, which is what is most important; however, after many decades of international aid, the problem of poverty remains unsolved while a large number of people have earned generous salaries from working in this sector. We can see that this association between helping and making money is problematic. Yes, the charities help, but how much and for how long, and who is truly benefiting? Is it acceptable for the charity to benefit its staff? If so, how should that look? People have to be paid; should they be penalized for wanting to help some of the world's poorest?

I've worked at a charity and earned a decent salary, so I'm not casting aspersions. We should be examining some of the processes in the world of international aid through the lens of results (or the lack thereof). We should be wondering how beneficial all the charitable activity is. We should also consider how the effort to end poverty is being affected by the charities' lack of trust in those they help to administer funds themselves. This systemically paternalistic way of thinking is condescending and oppressive; some of those being helped would have integrity in relation to using the funds; others wouldn't – as is the case with individuals in the West.

The association between the helpers and the helped is never straight-forward. Power dynamics are not straightforward: there are no perfect ways of standing with people to solve injustice. We should, however, explore our motives for wanting to do so, and focus more on whether we are truly helping and could, perhaps, do better.

9

A pack of privilege

The way we currently talk about, and understand, 'power', 'privilege' and 'allyship' makes me think that we are missing the nuances that make them helpful frames of reference. Instead, they seem to be immovable walls that hem us in. Having conversations at all is a step forwards. Nevertheless, our next steps must be to use these frames of reference to create pathways to change. Talking about privilege, especially White privilege, almost guarantees a defensive reaction from some, as does discussing power dynamics and allyship, which highlights a gap and the need for something to change. Regarding privilege, the first big obstacle to overcome is how to learn to understand it in a nuanced way.

Shuffle the pack

Just because you have an advantage doesn't mean that you know you have it.

My sister taught me to read at the age of four. Reading came fairly naturally to me and, at the age of five, when I started school, I didn't realize that I had an advantage over the children in my class who hadn't learnt to read. I raced through all the age-appropriate books with ease and moved on to more advanced ones. The fact that others struggled to read had no impact on me, and the fact that I found reading easy didn't affect them. However, I was struggling with other things at school, such as separation anxiety: I missed my mum and younger sister, who were at home. The teacher told my mum that, every day for that first week at school, I cried all day. But when my mum asked me how each day was, I bravely pretended that it was fine – at five years old!

The duality of my first experience of school wouldn't cause me to think that I had any advantage. If someone were to point out that I'd had a good start at school because I could read well, I would highlight my initial emotional difficulties as evidence that the situation was rather more complex. So it is with the advantages that we have in life. While we may not have to try as hard in one area, there may be immense difficulty in others. For some people, there may be more barriers and areas of struggle than ease.

To make a more accurate assessment of the areas I have to contend with in life, I like to consider all the advantages and disadvantages. First there's the physical realm: our bodies and the spaces that we inhabit; the homes we live in and where we work. Are we able-bodied? Do we have the ability to move through the world with ease? If not, how much does disability hold us back? Second, there's the mental realm: our minds and our mental health, to which is related the experience of our formative years. Were we not given enough? Were we left to fend for ourselves? Did we learn early that we had to work hard for the things we want? Alternatively, was everything given to us, preventing us from growing in grit and resilience? Where do we fit on the mental-health spectrum? How is our mental health and how does it affect our daily lives? We all have problems with our mental health at some point and, at times, mine hasn't been great. Third, there is the emotional realm: upbringing, past traumas and present experiences. Did we grow up loved, and feeling safe and secure? Were we abandoned and, as a result, are we insecure? Are we able to connect with and understand our own feelings? We have to consider these three major personal and internal factors before we even think about the external world: careers, friends, love interests and the rest.

We tend to think about advantage as encompassing a few obvious characteristics: race, gender and class. The truth is that advantage is a complex web that has many factors. We can't say that possessing one particular advantage makes everything fine. Even so, some advantages do make a big difference to how we experience life. When we break advantage down, it is like a pack of cards: some cards have a high value, but the value and meaning of each card also depend on the game we play. Sometimes, we don't need an ace; we need a two. Occasionally, we don't need hearts; we need clubs.

When I look at my life and all the privileges that I have had, and continue to have, I don't believe that, as a Black woman, I am at the bottom of the pile for everything. It's simply not true, but I can't speak for every Black woman and her circumstances. Not every White man has had or will have more opportunities than I have. But, in certain circumstances, White men will have had greater opportunities and better outcomes than I have, and they will have found it easier to achieve their goals simply because they are White and male. In general, there is an undoubted bias in their favour. However, if we drill down to individual circumstances, the way in which advantage works is not so simple. If you are born into a family that is economically disadvantaged, there are usually additional disadvantages: less physical space, possibly a nutritional deficit, and less access to books and technology, for example. But what if someone in an economically disadvantaged family works in a supermarket and receives discounts on food? What if a family member has spent years building up an extensive library that is easily accessible to the rest of the family? These factors will alter the level of perceived disadvantage.

A balanced view of advantage involves considering individual circumstances and variables. We might think that we can make generalizations about people who have been brought up by two parents but, if we were to take into account a variety of other factors, can we really? Those parents might have had a very dysfunctional relationship that damaged their children emotionally, causing repercussions for the latter in their adult relationships and careers. We have to make the caveat, when talking in general terms, that no group is monolithic and should not be treated as such.

The stories data tell

Data are helpful because they provide statistics. At the end of every statistic, however, is a person and therefore myriad things that may be measured. The human desire to categorize and pigeonhole means that we will never give up measuring. I'm not against measuring stuff; it is good to know, for example, whether your child is developing on a par with other children. But we know that single measurements don't ensure outcomes. For example, an above-average child may not receive the best marks or, as an adult, bag the most amazing job. Yet, as a society, we lower expectations for children from certain ethnic groups or family circumstances. We limit what we believe they can do and, by doing so in many cases, lower the children's own level of expectation.

We stick with hypotheses that lack nuance and which are usually rooted in our biases. We design very elaborate stories around those hypotheses while looking at data from an angle that supports our predetermined beliefs. There will always be those who fit the description, and who are highlighted as case studies that prove the theory. And then there are those who exceed expectations. Yet we keep squeezing young people into predetermined futures based on circumstances beyond their control. This way of organizing the world is extremely limiting for some, and it ensures that the status quo is preserved for others, especially because many of these hypotheses are based on sweeping generalizations. Rather than dismantling systemic obstacles, these beliefs can reinforce them by continually discouraging people who are already disadvantaged.

Immutable advantage?

It is a struggle to close the gap between where we are and where we could be when everyone is certain that it can never be done. We seem to be convinced that some advantages and disadvantages are so powerful that we are all at their mercy. In reality, they belong to an ideology that can be dismantled. It is an ideology that presents working-class Black boys with a low ceiling; it is an ideology that tells them they can achieve only certain things. It is a narrative that is flawed but powerful. When we think of advantage as part of the data that are fed into their potential futures, these boys are at a disadvantage. Nevertheless, advantage does not have to be a fixed, binary way of being. For each child who comes to school hungry and can't concentrate, there might be a teacher who provides breakfast every day, which could help to alter the expected outcome. These calculations and recalculations of types of privilege change throughout life.

The concept of how advantage or privilege might affect our chances in life is vividly illustrated by a video in which young people stand at a starting line before a race. They are asked to take a step forwards if they have two parents; then another step if their parents own their home; and so on.[1] On a rudimentary level, the exercise explains how advantage works. However, I believe that this method of explaining it is harmful for those taking part because it might limit or exacerbate how they see themselves and their potential. For those who think that they can never win because they are too far back, it reinforces an unhelpful way of thinking. Those at the front might feel special because their head start is more likely to help them to reach their goals. Alternatively, they might be deeply aware that they have little personal merit to warrant what they do have and so feel insecure and inadequate, despite their privilege.

Explaining privilege so simplistically allows all kinds of misconceptions to arise. After all, there might be other mitigating circumstances. For example, we might be able to take a step forwards because our parents are married, but do they get on? Are they in a healthy functioning relationship? Are we learning to live with double standards, in which outward appearances are considered more important than the truth of what goes on behind closed doors? We would have to take a step back if our parents should have separated long ago. Two parents are an advantage but with several caveats because life is grey rather than black and white. We might be better off with separated parents or one parent to minimize the effects of dysfunction. We might also have to consider whether our parents work all the time or have any addictions. This exercise could be repeated for every question asked in the video.

The measurements that we use as indicators of advantage haven't been reassessed for a long time. Some of the ways in which we categorize class and so on have changed. These days, we understand so much more about emotional, mental and spiritual factors and how they have an impact on our whole lives. (For example, while a lot of people still desire material wealth, many of us now know that it doesn't necessarily result in emotional or physical well-being.) Our thinking concerning privilege should include such factors. New indicators that do away with singular narratives and embrace complexity will enable us to see accurately whether we have advantages or disadvantages. This knowledge will help us to improve our understanding of one another, which would result in informed conversations and better outcomes for all.

Privilege has caveats

In an ideal world, all the different kinds of advantage would be easily measured and understood, and perfectly aligned to guaranteed outcomes. However, life isn't perfect and the current understanding of privilege allows us to believe that we have more disadvantages or advantages than we really do. We tend to disregard factors that indicate people are struggling despite their supposed advantages. Take, for example, celebrities and all that they have – the money and the adoration – yet the outcomes for some of them are substance abuse, addictions, floundering relationships, bankruptcy, fragile mental health and, in some cases, suicide. We also tend to discount the fact that sometimes things aren't as they appear, which allows, for example, privileged people to be treated as victims. There is often little sympathy for those who have all the advantages and yet are 'never happy'. Conversely, there might not be any help for those who don't stand a chance. These factors are detrimental to the functioning of society, and how we view and help one another. They lead to resentment and misunderstanding because groups of people are forced to prove that they are the most deserving among the disadvantaged, in turn forcing those who want to help to make unedifying choices. Rather than looking at privilege as an ever-growing points-based list, we have to acknowledge the elements that detract from and lessen the advantages, so we can arrive at a true measure that will help us to find solutions.

Forever help

Until we look at privilege in a closer and more nuanced way, we cannot begin to tackle inequality. We have made privilege the cure and the curse that keep us in an equidistant holding pattern. This pattern arises from our accepting that some have privilege, others don't and there's nothing we can do about it; the scales of privilege remain rusted and fixed. That perceived helplessness gives us the excuse to do nothing about issues we consider immovable. So we continue to reach down and support others, or even try to raise them a little higher, but we can never do quite enough to level the mountain of privilege.

Entitled to receive gratitude

The truth is that, in many cases, we like to help people. We like the gap and to have the advantage. It affirms the story that we like about ourselves. There is a well-known proverb that says, 'Give a man a fish, and you feed him for a day. Teach a man to fish, and you feed him for a lifetime.'[2] For some, giving people fish every time they're hungry is satisfying. That way, they look to us for the things they need. In fact, they need *us*. Without *our* providing the fish, how would they survive? They wouldn't, we think, so we blind ourselves to many facts: they would probably prefer things to be fairer and to be able to do their own fishing, with their own equipment. They would probably rather not have to ask for help every time they were hungry or have to wait for aid. Instead of allowing people the dignity of looking after themselves, we want to provide for them and receive all the associated gratitude. We pretend that what we do is for others but it's really for us. This gap is one that will never be closed: we are forever helping and forever being thanked – the helped and the helpers forever stuck in a power imbalance.

Entitled to receive help

One aspect of this unhealthy pattern is that there are people who seem to enjoy it: they don't believe that they can be self-sufficient or they don't want to learn how to be. They have no intention of finding a way to escape their situation. They say to themselves, 'Well, I've never had a fishing rod, so I've never learnt to fish.' They want us to come every day so that they can demand fish. They have always lacked fish, so they believe that those who have fish are obliged to share. Out of necessity, an expectation – or even a sense of entitlement – is born. This behaviour mimics that of a parent-and-child relationship. Infantilization is a perpetual conse-quence of the exercising of privilege: one party knows what's best while refusing to see the person he or she 'helps' as equal. 'Forever helpers', who unconsciously believe that they are inherently superior, treat others as inherently incapable of helping themselves, when, in reality, the perceived helplessness is often owing to a lack of opportunity. The answer cannot be to want or need to give or receive help continually. On both sides, there should be a rejection of this current status quo.

Privilege, consent and self-determination

Privilege used well offers people support, with consent and with the understanding that some teaching might be necessary, and then steps back when appropriate. The abuse of privilege can result in learned helplessness in the recipients of aid, rather than in encouraging them to change the cards in their pack.

It would be ideal if improving our situation were to require only skills and talent, but we would also need a whole set of societal norms and tools to which only select groups have access. Yet these advantages have become essential to us. The status quo with regard to privilege has made some of us beggars because we think we don't have any privilege at all. We have to reject this thinking, especially because anyone can start from small beginnings and use the advantage of self-determination to better his or her lot.

Keeping analysis relevant

'White privilege: Unpacking the invisible knapsack'[3] was a paper written in 1989 to explore how being White garners invisible advantages. We should assess whether the paper is as relevant as it once was because much has changed in the intervening years, so we have to carry out our own similar social and cultural analyses. For example, we've learnt more about our bodies in the past 30 years; the way we look after them has changed. Also, when we consider the work of feminist or civil rights campaigners from years, decades or even centuries ago, we must use it with the caveat that times have changed.

Any work, academic or otherwise, reflects its time and, since 1989, many of us have taken steps to live, love and work together. Progress in these areas has been achieved because people from disadvantaged groups have spoken up, protested and made space for the necessary changes, and because others have used their privilege, power and platforms to speak up for change. Privilege will continue to have a role in change, but it also has a role in preserving systemic injustices. We must continually reassess the impact of privilege and what it means in context – that is, in our time, and with regard to our current laws and attitudes. We must also think about what it means in the contexts of different countries. The ways ethnicity, gender, sexuality and privilege are viewed elsewhere do not necessarily equate to the ways they are seen in the West; they never have. Different cultures in various eras have prized or rejected a variety of factors.

A non-White-centred world

An advantage I had growing up was a strong sense of pride in my culture, in Black history and in my knowledge of them. As a result, the way I see myself and my place in the world has always been through a lens of self-determination. I have never wanted to be anything other than a Black woman because I wasn't taught to see my colour and sex as hindrances. To be brought up without imbibing a dominant culture, which does not always see us as we are, helps us to be resilient when that dominant culture refuses to recognize us. This kind of advantage cannot be underestimated. Nevertheless, it doesn't mean that I have remained unaffected by the way mainstream society views me. I understand that White privilege exists but I don't allow it to have an impact on every single outcome.

When we look at White privilege in a binary way, we ignore the evidence; we have blind spots around it. When we uncritically absorb the singular narrative of what that particular advantage allows and prevents, we hinder progress for everyone. We elevate its status by saying that nothing else matters as much or we can never ameliorate it. If I were to choose to view White male privilege as an insurmountable obstacle through my lens (that of a woman who is Black), I would assume that nothing would make a difference; I would be irredeemably oppressed. It wouldn't matter that I grew up in a home my married parents owned. It would make no difference that those parents loved me very much and provided ample opportunities for me to pursue my chosen career. It wouldn't matter at all that I had a middle-class upbringing and benefited from the associated opportunities. The binary-advantage narrative says that none of those particular advantages will ever matter because I am Black and a woman.

You must excuse me for rejecting this line of thought, but I believe we can accept that racial privilege is a huge problem while understanding it affects different people to varying degrees because other privileges are in play. For example, the social class that I belong to has had a significant impact on the choices I've made and the things I've done. I believe that we must look at privilege in tandem with the sum total of our individual circumstances.

Some might say that I am denying the magnitude of racial privilege. There are those who have suggested that I should see how I would feel if I were to have a negative encounter with the police – then I'd know that I was Black! That may well be true, but does it mean that I have to accept my life will never be all it could be because I'm not White? For me, that attitude makes someone else's prejudices the centre of my life experience. I am unwilling to relinquish the power that I have, and I reject the idea that somehow I must seek someone else's permission to achieve. When I reflect on the constrained thinking around White privilege, and its effect on our ability to see where we could be, I'm reminded of the mental slavery that Bob Marley and the Wailers sang about in 'Redemption Song'. I acknowledge that if I were to be stopped by the police, it might be an unpleasant experience, but I have never been stopped by them, so I don't know how it feels. However, I do believe that I haven't been invited to job interviews because of my ethnicity. At work, for being as direct as a White man might be, I have been labelled aggressive because others wouldn't accept such assertiveness from me, a Black woman. I am fully aware of the pain caused by these types of assumption. Even so, they have comprised only parts of my experience rather than my whole experience. I cannot judge my life solely on unpleasant moments. I have had a career that I have found satisfying, and many people have thanked me for being direct and honest, and for helping them and their careers to grow.

Privilege is a complex and sprawling pack of cards. Whether you win the card game depends on which one you're playing and the value of the cards in your hand. There have been times when I've been quite sure that being a Black woman has served me well and has been an advantage. Does that make me bad at my job? No. It just means that when I was employed, my employers were looking for a certain factors and I fitted the bill. This realization would diminish my view of myself only if I were to let it.

The odds have been stacked in the favour of White men for a long time. However, we can also see that things have been and are changing. Nevertheless, we are still far from a society in which the sexes and different races are generally equal. We don't live in an ideal world, but our hopes, dreams, and our own advantages and disadvantages can be used to bring that ideal to fruition.

The negative reaction to diversity schemes has much to do with people protecting their interests, opportunities and privilege. Popular language and slogans tell us, in basic terms, that we can do anything and be anything we want, with little or no effort, which is profoundly misleading. No one is good at everything. Sometimes, the things we want, but are not willing to work for, don't materialize, and we wrongly attribute this failure to the obstacle of privilege. By doing so, privilege is assumed to be a far stronger driving force than it truly is.

In the end, preserving and acquiring privilege are all about material gain because ours is a capitalist society. An accrual of advantages help us to experience life in a better way. We should want everyone to have a comfortable life, which, for some, means amassing excess wealth. Financial inequalities seem particularly unfair and can make the discussion around privilege especially fraught. If we were to take money out of the equation, we might see clearly what truly has to be different. The question is, what are we really fighting to change?

Loaded language

Words such as 'privilege' have become so loaded that they are almost slurs. If we want everyone involved in discourses of change to appreciate nuances, we have to think about the language we use.

The narrative around privilege unfolds something like this: White man – strong and bad; Black person – victim and helpless. This story tells us that White men are the problem and we can't overcome their oppressiveness. Can there be a conversation that starts with this insinuation that ends well? Also, to a White man who may not have thought about his advantages and how they've helped him, this idea is very challenging: he is not who he thinks he is, and we (non-White people) have noticed the gap because we know that we share few, if any, of his advantages. On many levels, this will be profoundly uncomfortable for him. Very few people can accommodate realizing something so significant in a split second, and fewer still will change their behaviour instantaneously as a result. For most, recognizing and accepting the gap between what we believe and what is true, and then choosing to change, takes time; it's a journey.

The conversation around privilege is loaded because we have no choice in terms of where we're born or what we're born into. When you think that something is not your fault and yet someone is laying blame at your door, defensiveness is, inevitably, the first reaction. We must consider whether making someone feel bad for what can't be helped is the best point at which to start an interaction. We must remember that we are all human. In some cases, those who are privileged and have a head start in life have simply never thought to look back. If that is you, then here is an invitation to see what's behind you and why.

Ours is a population in which the members of each ethnicity, sex, class and so on have varying abilities. But, when we take a moment to consider, we can see that most of us are not proportionally and fairly represented at every level of society. So clearly, somewhere, advantage is playing a role in the current status quo. We can hope that the situation will improve, even when it is with five steps forward and two steps back. The trajectory can only be upwards. To ensure progress, we all need to think about how complicit we are in thinking, acting, speaking and behaving as if things will never change.

As a Black woman, I am, at times, dismayed by the discourse on both sides. I believe that hope and a new vision are needed for change. However, all sides of all debates seem to continually validate the hopelessness of the situation, which leads to stagnating debates and slow progress. We spend too much time in circular conversations about peripheral issues, which prevent us from tackling major systemic injustices and bringing about true change.

Who has the mic?

When talking about privilege and advantage, everyone has a different understanding. However, when the voices championing progress are not comfortable or confident enough to have difficult conversations, and when they won't acknowledge that complex situations require nuanced solutions, the people who most need the change are the ones who lose. Discussion is never cracked wide open by moderates who want to understand both sides of an argument and be fair. It is cracked open by polarized parties. The public space of discourse is often occupied by people with hard-line views, many of whom have no intention of changing their perspectives because, apart from anything else, they are paid to take a strong stance on certain subjects by media companies.

These disparate positions can result in fiery debates that are great for broadcasting. While it's wonderful that some of these much needed discussions are given air time to bring certain issues to the notice of the public, most broadcasters only want to highlight those issues that are topical. Media professionals are not necessarily interested in helping to solve long-term problems; they are storytellers, not peace-brokers or policy-makers.

For those of us who belong to UK minorities, it's great to see people defending and championing our communities on TV or radio. But we must also recognize that those who have the opportunity to speak have some kind of advantage or they wouldn't be invited to stand in front of a camera or sit before a microphone. In addition, they are coming to the debate with their own biases and preferences; they aren't necessarily going to talk about what matters to us, and so it's important to view them with this understanding. These caveats illustrate why advantage is very tricky.

People are invited to speak on issues that affect marginalized people, and they do, but speaking is different from actually changing things. We must ask what the role of these representatives, or middlepersons, is. They agitate the people they are debating with; they agitate the people they are aligned with (and are paid to do so in the columns they write and sometimes during their appearances on TV) but what changes for the marginalized community? Often, a Black person (or someone who identifies as Black) who has certain advantages won't necessarily understand the needs of every less advantaged member of the community for which they speak. Some people who talk a lot about privilege are privileged within their own communities; they may need to mind their gaps. We must all look out for double standards, especially in ourselves.

All of us have work to do in this area. To hear that we haven't recognized the advantages we have over others is, of course, challenging and confrontational. However, we must begin to examine our lives to identify our advantages and how they have accumulated to enhance our experiences. And then we should consider others. Acknowledging our advantages shouldn't result in our pitying those who have less. After all, many of our advantages have been given rather than earned. Once we've identified those received advantages, we can identify the ones that we have earned. And we might have to acknowledge that the advantages we have earned resulted from the ones that we were given in the first place!

Black *and* privileged

Just because you are Black does not mean that you are not privileged.

The current understanding of privilege supposes that every single White person we pass on the street is guaranteed better outcomes than we are, simply because of the colour of his or her skin. This belief is not true. For example, a White, poor, jobless woman is usually immediately considered disadvantaged. There are a great many variations with regard to advantage and disadvantage. The intersection of race, gender and class must be considered together; they are the three major areas of privilege that have an impact on the way each of us is seen, especially as their importance ebbs and flows in particular contexts. I have certain advantages because of my birth, upbringing and the locations in which I grew up. To those received advantages, I have added others through nurturing natural talent to build a career. Writing a book or being able to tweet is an advantage: I can't say that I'm silenced when I have platforms from which to speak. Of course, my highlighting my own position in society does not negate that there are those who are racist, sexist and so on. I do not deny that some people go out of their way to hold others back. However, I believe that most of those perceived as disadvantaged remain so because others with greater advantages just don't care enough.

In many cases, historic advantage gaps have not been closed, but not necessarily because unkind people are operating from a place of hate.

Unconscious bias can probably be more accurately identified as the reason the gap still exists. It's a useful term, but only to a point because it's one behind which we hide. I would argue that once we recognize the existence of unconscious bias, we should examine ourselves for it, as well as acknowledging our blind spots. But, to be blunt, most of us don't. For example, I'll barely, if ever, think about being able-bodied – until an event or situation forces me to confront the fact that I am.

Part of the problem in our communication with others is that, when we participate in these conversations, we assume others know we have deep pain. Of course, they probably don't know. Apart from anything else, most people spend most of their time thinking about their own pain. Once others are aware, however, we enter different territory. We must remember that our world view is just that – ours. I remember a painful conversation that I had while working at a charity. The woman with whom I had the exchange told me that I couldn't lead my team properly if I didn't care deeply about a particular area of injustice, the one on which she happened to be working. I replied that I would educate myself about it. I also said that I did care but not as much as she did, and it was likely I never would because I was very passionate about another area.

We must become attuned to this fact that different people have different passions. We can't all care deeply about everything all the time. There are enough people, who are passionate about different injustices, for us to focus exclusively on the areas to which we are called. Some might say that it's my privilege which allows me to walk away from certain injustices; perhaps they're right. However, we must tolerate others who care about different areas of injustice and recognize that different injustices are topical at different times, and their importance in the public consciousness ebbs and flows. If we think that the injustice we believe to be the most vital must always be at the forefront of everyone else's minds, we will be very disappointed. The injustice we care about is not necessarily being ignored because of privilege but because people are choosing other priorities.

One of my aims in life is to prioritize the societal progression of Black people. The way I choose to do so won't necessarily make sense to those involved in different fights. In fact, they might think that I'm dismissive of their causes. I am not; I care about many issues, but there are particular ones to which I am strongly drawn. At some point, my priority will be topical and, when that time comes, I want to do as much as I can to publicize and address the injustices around it.

We all have preferences and we all prioritize our preferences. We can't expect other people to care as deeply about certain issues as we do; they might not think as much about our priorities as we would like, but that's all right. We must resist the temptation to shame people or make them feel guilty for not sharing our passions. When an injustice is raised, however, we should expect people who call themselves decent and reasonable to join us in taking action to bring about change. Often, when those who have certain advantages finally engage with an issue, they will use their privilege as well as they can to redress the balance.

10
Power truths

I always try to remember that there are three sides to every story: yours, mine and the truth. As much as I value honesty, not every truth has to be told. I have experienced the pain of being told a harsh truth. The truth can be very ugly, so, occasionally, relationships don't survive the truth-telling. It explains why, when the truth is required, we tend to hide behind smiles and polite words.

One of the biggest lies relating to disadvantaged people is that they have no agency.[1] This belief makes it easy to maintain the status quo, not only for people with bad intentions but also for those who don't think or who oversimplify. Also, this myth is repeated by those who like to be continual helpers, who might be described as having a saviour or Jesus complex. When the people we help don't have any agency, they can never, ever help themselves. No matter what, they will always need help; they will always need us.

The truth about agency is that some people enjoy having power over others, which is human, so there's nothing to see here. The ugly part is that most of us would deny we have a desire or, in some cases, need to control situations and others. We want this agency because it keeps our stories intact; we can control events to allow them to unfold in a way that we find favourable.

Most of us prefer to control rather than be controlled, which is why entrepreneurship is attractive to many. Young people, especially, feel attracted to being in charge of their own professional lives: they can work the hours they want and be their own boss, so they take the plunge. After a while, they might realize how difficult being self-employed is to maintain; so many throw in the towel and find salaried work (including me, though I'm not so young). Most of us do not know that. We look at those who work for themselves with envy; they seem so 'free'. Many of us want that freedom because we don't like being told what to do and being made to do it. This situation is worse when our line managers are people we don't like or respect. As noted, however, the reality of self-employment is usually different from the fantasy: those who work for themselves work harder than those who clock in and out because the stakes are higher. Being in control and having complete responsibility for our lives is a normal desire, but it takes effort.

I first moved out from home as a teenager, but I returned within a few weeks. I discovered that freedom with no money and a dearth of the comforts that I was used to wasn't actually freedom. Even so, my own internal agency was dying for a taste of independence. Living at home meant that I had to abide by my parents' rules, whereas I wanted to live life on my own terms. Other people desire similar freedom, but they see that the price of using their agency is one of personal responsibility, so they stay at home or return home, as I did. However, their relinquishing of independence doesn't mean that they don't have the agency to become independent. Rather, they choose not to do so or, for various reasons, didn't think that they could.

The rules

When we live in somebody else's home there might be things we want to do that he or she would rather we didn't. It could be anything from wearing shoes inside to smoking or even tidying up. The person who owns or rents the space dictates the rules. Even when he or she is very generous and says, 'Take what you like. Do what you like', there are always limits. If you are wise, you will know what those are and work within them. But you still have a bit of your own agency – within set boundaries. We play along because we are aware of the consequences of exceeding the limits of our agency in a space that isn't ours. Those consequences might include being kicked out or not invited back. So we *choose* to deny ourselves to stay in that space.

The shift of power

In the same way, everyone in society has agency – that is, their own internal powerhouse – that enables them to choose and make decisions.

The quickest way to give power away is to think that you don't have it. Most people have power in a number of ways but when we speak about it collectively, we often think that we don't have it, or that we can't or shouldn't assert it. We can look at power and think of it as being related to material and monetary advantages but it is incorrect to think about agency in only that way.

Power depends on many factors in modern society. We see those who are marginalized increasingly making themselves heard. The Me Too and Black Lives Matter movements are recent examples of people speaking out strongly and loudly about long-term oppression. Of course, digital technology has also played a large part in democratizing the use of agency.

There are things to be wary of in this conversation. Social media provide an important space in today's culture, but they are not universally used or all powerful. It can be easy to think that they take the temperature of a nation; election results, for example, seem to tell us as much. But, we also know that social media can be echo chambers, so we are unlikely to see many, if any, views that oppose ours, unless we actively choose to do so.

Having said that, long before social media existed, there were movements initiated by disadvantaged people. We have always found ways to gather and make our voices heard. Technology has simply made it easier for us all to find like-minded people and to organize campaigns or protests. Many recent uprisings around the world were organized through social media, such as private messaging groups, even in places ruled by very oppressive regimes.

The fact that these movements could gain traction shows us that agency isn't found only in the places we would expect. So why do so many people believe that they have no power? How do we find ways of communicating that we all have it? How can we communicate that the misuse of it, and reallocating it on others' behalf, is the problem? Personally, I've discovered the issue is not that I didn't have any agency but other people thought I didn't, or shouldn't, have it. Once, when I used my agency in a professional capacity, there was palpable resistance – mostly from White women and men of various races.

Shameless

I have observed two ways in which agency might be misused. First, people who know that they are powerful engage in nepotism, favouritism and so on. This overt misuse of agency is often shameless because those who do so know that others are powerless to stop it. It's a type of oppression that maintains the status quo for a long time. The lack of denial actually strengthens the hands of those doing the oppressing. They don't even pretend that it's not happening or that they think it's unacceptable. They want us to know that it doesn't matter what we do or say because the situation is what it is.

Second, there are those who pretend that they don't have any agency while at the same time exercising it. These types of people are particularly dangerous because they are Machiavellian. They will always say that they didn't know what they were doing or continually claim that they have no power. Much of what they do is explained away, rather than addressed, because their use of power is covert rather than overt. After all, we can use something only if we have it.

So the two types of the misuse of agency are toxic for different reasons.

Cancelled or called-out?

Calling someone out for misusing agency is very powerful, as we often see on social media. Some people say that cancel culture[2] doesn't exist; nevertheless, we do see the strength and pressure of online crowds. Although no longer physical mobs with pitchforks and flaming torches, this multitude is able to silence the powerful and not-so-powerful in ways that were once inconceivable. However, those who silence others on social media often remain unaccountable for what they say because they have 'no power'. It's an interesting narrative: when we have no agency, we cannot be expected to take personal responsibility for our opinions and behaviour. Without power, how can we offend?

We must be able to discuss these complex dynamics in order to move forwards. We must acknowledge the shifting of agency, and how it's a line in the sand that has been redrawn. On those occasions when we talk about agency, we do so in a way that is easy to articulate: we have no agency; therefore, no agency means a straightforward dynamic. We avoid focusing on its complexity, particularly now that we have a variety of means of communicating. Apart from the issue of complexity, another reason we don't engage well regarding agency on social media is that, ironically, we fear being cancelled ourselves.

Technology has helped to democratize agency. Organizations fire people and change marketing campaigns not necessarily because of company policy but because of the agency of groups of people online, even though social media are not universal and do not reach all their customers or clients. So, if we believe that the limits of agency haven't been redefined, we need to think again. We must consider how types of power beget power of opposite kinds. The silencing of a group of people often drives them and their views underground. In those places, they gather; aggrieved and frustrated at being silenced, they return a stronger force, more capable of standing firm in the face of opposition. The loss of freedom to share thoughts and opinions freely has caused dangerous fringe groups to reorganize and become more vocal. It might also explain why populism is on the rise.

On digital platforms, it is increasingly difficult to disagree openly with others without being labelled as some sort of bigot. On the one hand, some rhetoric absolutely is rooted in bigotry. On the other, some commentators are merely exploring topics that they don't understand; alternatively, they do understand the subject but disagree with the majority view, which is their right. We must allow for the reality that people understand the facts presented but choose to see them a different way. Policing one another's thoughts is not the answer; we all want to be free to think what we want.

How can we recognize that agency is shifting? Once, in private, a colleague very calmly told me that he was scared of me. Usually, when people are frightened they don't feel empowered enough to tell the person concerned directly. For my part, I believed that my colleague was making a power play. In effect, he wanted me to change my behaviour to do what he wanted.

When more people recognize their agency and use it wisely, the world will be a better place. We have to recognize both the positive and the destructive ways in which agency can be used.

Is there a new order?

I can understand why people don't think that they have any power; it has been in the hands of the few for so long. We have yet to fully catch up with the shift in culture, and what it means for us and the way we interact with one another. The ugly truth concerning those of us who suddenly discover our agency is that we can be brutal. Sometimes, we use our new-found power for revenge – to right perceived wrongs – rather than for seeking justice and equality; but, to preserve our standing as good and reasonable people, we say that we are fighting for justice and nothing else. We see this gap in the tweets and posts of those belonging to fringe movements, and we can read between the lines of some of the rhetoric. For my part, I make it crystal-clear that I'm not against men; I'm for women. I'm not against White people; I am for Black people.

We can see that, when power shifts, language moves with it. The word 'racism' has been redefined in a cultural sense to mean 'prejudice plus power'. This redefining of the word means there is the opinion that racism affects people in only one direction. However, the original definition of the word is clear – racism can affect anyone of any race. The agency that people have to redefine the meaning of a word cannot be underestimated; it shows power. Of course, not everyone agrees with the redefinition, which exacerbates the problem of miscommunication.

To conclude: while people might *feel* powerless, it isn't true that they are.

The Wild West

There are no real rules in social-media spaces. The communities started out flat, without hierarchy and organization. As time has gone on, we have seen the platforms evolving, especially in terms of hierarchy. Elements such as verification[3] and powerful hashtags, which become full-blown movements, are beginning to define a structure. I believe that, eventually, social media will settle into a new way of being. They are young: they have been a serious online presence for fewer than 20 years. They are still babies, and we haven't worked out the best way to interact with them and with one another on them. These things take time. So, in

138

real terms, the power shift has happened before we've had the chance to explore what it means.

The cart is always before the horse when it comes to shifts in culture. If we were to have the chance to observe the power shift, we would probably interact with others in the spaces a little differently. As always, cultural intelligence takes time to develop; we will only really see the full picture with hindsight. The power of cancel (or call-out) culture may actually force changes in the end, as people become more cautious about what they say. When we know that our words might eventually come back to haunt us, we will tread carefully.

Social media are not the world, but they are places where we can observe group behaviour. They give us a fascinating insight into how we behave – how we truly behave rather than how we'd like to.

Comfortable conflict

The thing about agency is that – whether we deny it, don't see that we have it or use it to dominate – others can probably see more clearly than we do how much we have and how we use it. That is why we usually don't acknowledge agency in ourselves; it's much easier to examine what other people are doing with theirs. Currently, the biggest power play of all is that of commentators co-opting the past to excuse the way they use their power now. It is uncomfortable to witness. Many people accept that the world is unbalanced and things have to change. However, the pendulum is swinging too far in a different direction, resulting in another form of suppression.

The way in which online agency is currently wielded could be described as puritanical. Instead of preaching religious (self-)righteousness, social-media commentators trumpet their moral (self-)righteousness at being on the side of everyone they consider to be marginalized. It seems that defending those we believe to be excluded gives us carte blanche to discuss certain other groups in any way we like, particularly White people, heterosexuals, Christians and men. These types of people are commonly described in ways that marginalized groups would never accept. When we want to use our power for justice, how can we be sure that we are not imitating the (deplorable) tactics of those with whom we disagree? One of many examples of the misuse of agency I've seen online involves discussions about abolishing the prison system. The conversations often revolve around the belief that the prison system is not effective for rehabilitating people. Some of those involved will cancel others for disagreeing with them, and they will vehemently encourage others to shun those 'disagreeable' people too.

We have to decide how we want to use our new, democratic agency. For instance, we should think about the consequences when someone is permanently excluded from a platform. By being cancelled, might he or she lose a means of earning a living? To have the agency, as part of a group, to cause someone to lose a job – even when we believe it to be deserved – is heady. This illustrates how, in terms of social equity, there has been a huge shift in the dynamics of power. We have to be comfortable with conflict, but the path we are currently on will end in collision. These culture wars can become very nasty, and no side truly wins.

We could argue that any power, other than that bestowed by capitalist wealth, doesn't count; essentially, most people want to achieve some kind of financial stability or even success. But I think it does count. If we truly want progress and to improve communication, we have to acknowledge all the ways in which power is evident in online discourse. The point is not about taking power away from anyone. Rather, it's about choosing not to duel but to collaborate, and to use our collective agency to create a better society. Those on both sides of a conversation tend to have the kind of power the other side would like, so we should work at respecting the power we each have, rather than using verbal brute force to flatten each other.

Different people have different attitudes to power. Some don't care about power in certain contexts. For example, they might not have much agency at work: that's all right – they are happy to turn up and collect their pay. Also, there might be something that they could kick up a fuss about, but they choose not to because it has little to do with their reason for going to work.

Some people bide their time to use their power; they enter a place and build support before wielding it to achieve their aims, a little like a stroppy child in a shop who knows that it's embarrassing its parents. The child understands that it has more power to manipulate in the shop than at home. There's something in us that knows where and when to act for maximum effect.

The social-media power dynamic is one with which we must continue to tinker.

Equilibrium

In its own way, this new power is stifling and oppressive. Someone can be cast out not only for doing the wrong thing but also for thinking the wrong thing. There is often no argument or redress. What if the views we held without censure 20 or 30 years ago were considered beyond the pale today? We might lose income or our jobs. In some cases, such an outcome might be appropriate but, in others, it wouldn't be. We are, all of us, imperfect people, so who has the right to decide which are the correct thoughts and opinions? It's no longer in the gift of the people who traditionally decided such things.

Once upon a time, only quiet power ruled the world. It was (and still is) hidden behind various thrones. We didn't (and still don't) know the names of those wielding this discreet power; we could only (and still do) speculate about their strategies and tactics. The new, democratized power, however, is very vocal; now we know many names and there are few secrets. Technology has allowed people who are sometimes nameless, faceless and silent to release details about those who are in the public eye. So, ironically, those behind leaks of information, who demand full accountability from the authorities, stay hidden. Their excuse for doing so is to increase their agency to allow them to reveal more. Surely, that is how the old, quiet power used to (and still does) behave. There might be some new masters but the old tactics remain. Power does this to us because we are all human. We operate in the gap between who we are and what we believe we're doing: we play hide and seek with the truth, knowing that everyone else will eventually become bored. Now more than ever, people's increasingly short attention spans allow those who play this game to get away with it.

An equilibrium of power is what we should all be striving for: that is, most people being able to share most of their thoughts without fear or favour. The question has always been whether something is too extreme, too far out on the fringe to be shared; whether it is genuinely too offensive. It is tough to work out because power has, for so long been in the hands of a few and has not been shared. Just like those who have new money and those who have old money, the people with old power and those with new power must learn to communicate; shutting down and shaming each other will get us nowhere.

To negate someone's opinion by trotting out the old line that 'everyone' thinks in a certain way is a cowardly approach to debate. It prevents the forensic analysis of an argument. If those who hold new power want to be taken seriously, their ideas must be held up to scrutiny. They should be able to accept criticism as well as dish it out, but the allure of online agency is the ease of avoiding criticism, and of being able to offer a view without any opposition. Others must be able to push back, however: that is democracy. We have already been subjected to untouchable power for so long that it would be a shame to leave one kind of dictatorship for another. If the true goal of commentators on social media were to be a new world where power were shared equitably, then the current tactics would need tweaking. Also, those who have traditionally held power would have to recognize that times have changed and initiate sharing some of their power.

There are people who are always convinced that they are right; the ones who speak in absolutes, preferring not to harbour doubt or consider nuances. The unwavering presumption that they are always right is overbearing. With the democratization of power that social media have provided, we have a window of opportunity to bring about change. But we will waste that opportunity if we refuse to be wrong, fail to disagree well and compromise, and use our agency to prevent a change of direction. Like money, agency, in and of itself, is not bad. What matters is how we put it to work. Those who use power well examine their motives: 'Am I using my energy or agency in a harmful way? How is what I'm doing bringing actual change? Is it bringing change? Can it bring change?'

Are we David or Goliath?

It is challenging to think that we are part of the problem of power; that in exercising our power, we might be trampling on someone else. No one wants to think of themselves in that way. In every David-and-Goliath scenario, most people think of themselves as David, even those you wouldn't expect to do so. Not many people want to be seen as Goliath, who was a bully, a monster and, ultimately, defeated. But some of the tactics the 'weak' use to bring down the 'strong' are those of the bully. What keeps us from assessing our use of power properly is the fear that we might be the aggressors. We don't want to admit that we are behaving in a way that we dislike. This point should not be used to shame others into goodness; self-examination must take place on all sides. The work must be done by everyone.

When our agency is used for good, we should try to replicate the result and invite more people to share in it.

Does David become Goliath?

'What will be done with the power?' is as important a question as 'Who has the power?' When power is wrested successfully from a dominant group, it can result in the exchange of one type of oppression for another. An exploration of the history of the past century or two shows this to be the case: repressive regimes are swept away only to be replaced by something just as bad or worse. People's revolutions can turn into blood-soaked terrors; people's heroes can become dictators.

Following a people's revolution, it might be difficult to govern by committee; so someone takes charge. The power dynamic is no longer about all being in it together, fighting side by side; a champion becomes the master and the relationship with the people changes. Before, the leader was merely campaigning; now he or she is governing: these are two very different ways of being and relating to people. Now, can that person who spoke truth to power receive the truth? After all, the person who calls out injustice may not necessarily be a just person. For instance, South Africa's Nelson Mandela is probably the only high-profile example of someone who successfully made the transition from being a campaigner against injustice to a leader who governed justly. However, the transition from campaigner to just leader for Myanmar's Aung Sung Suu Kyi has been rather less noteworthy and, for many, disappointing.

It's important to recognize the forms of injustice that exist within us, and to be open to changing them as well as calling out other people's injustice. We can only keep power under control as long as we understand that, with it, we can be as out of control as anyone else, and that we may be tempted to reach past equality to grasp dominance, when the opportunity arises. The moral high ground can never be claimed by a critic who refuses to be criticized. We must be open to criticism because believing that we are never wrong is power out of control; never having to listen is a symptom of dictatorship.

However, there is the legitimate type of leadership that calls for tough and unpopular decisions, and which requires a vision that others are yet to see – all for the greater good. For example, my parents dictated to me a lot for my good. If they hadn't dictated to me for my good but for their own, it would have been a destructive use of power. If we were to use our power for self-validation, it would be a misuse of power. If we were to campaign for issues just to make a living, it could lead to a misuse of power. If we were to act in ways that we wouldn't if money weren't involved, it would be a misuse of power. If we were to fight for causes to gain power and not because we believe, it would be a misuse of power.

Some misuses of power cause ripple effects out there in the world; sometimes a misuse of power causes ripple effects in us. At times, we forget that the things we do to others affect us: we can become very desensitized or we may come to dislike ourselves, both of which may be harmful when we have power over others.

I suspect that the biggest misuse of power arises when we feel insecure. We often think that some people mistreat others because they hate them or want to use them. It's not that simple. Those who feel good about themselves and who have a strong sense of self rarely misuse power. An abuse of power is a symptom of something deeper. The question we should ask ourselves is why, at times, we have misused our power. We might have done so because we view others as weaker or inferior in some way.

A boss can be insecure about his or her position because he or she lacks training for the role, because of poor performance or owing to pressure from superiors. Equally, just because someone is a boss doesn't mean his or her subordinates believe that he or she is their superior. It is quite common for some people to think that they are cleverer than their leaders. They'll often band with others who feel a similar way. This can happen for several reasons, which can include race and gender. It might be because of a personality clash. Sometimes, it is because the boss wants to change either the way the employees work or the shape of the team. In these situations, power can be fluid with regard to who has it and why.

When it comes to power we must expand our understanding of what it is and how it works. For example, I remember someone who cried when I corrected her. She threatened to post her version of our interaction on Facebook. In effect, she was saying, 'Do what I want or I'll tell everyone what you did and make you look bad.' She was wielding the power that she thought she had because, of course, no one wants to look bad. This kind of threatening behaviour is often used because it is effective; power is not only of the Goliath kind – large, boastful, loud and carrying on – it might involve merely telling someone that we'll do something to his or her detriment if that person doesn't do what we want.

Emotional manipulation is unhelpful

Another type of power is one that I term 'emotional manipulation', when facts are distorted to match feelings. It's a tactic that is used more and more frequently. No one can tell anyone else how they feel or how to feel. Feelings are personal. Feelings aren't facts and, because of that, I know them to be bad managers when we let them control our behaviour.

Statements such as 'Silence is violence' (which is used to manipulate people into speaking up on issues) fall into the category of emotional manipulation. There are many reasons why people might not voice an opinion in public. To speak up from a place of guilt and shame is not a helpful tactic in the long term. At a certain point, it might seem that a cause gains a lot of support but, when the time comes for real change, the support won't be there because it was founded on emotional manipulation. It is best not to use moral or emotional power to make people do things they don't want to do.

Examples of this are taking the knee and posting black squares on social media to show support for Black Lives Matter. Many people believed that others would think they were racist if they didn't make these gestures; then, a while later, those who did were chastised for not taking any concrete action to bring about change. It's a misuse of power

145

to use a crowd's agency to force people to prove their morality – that they are on the 'right' side – because these coerced gestures are nothing more than empty tokens that change nothing.

Can the oppressed be unjust?

A difficult topic to explore is that of believing people who are victims of injustice can't be unjust themselves. It is not a given that we are purified by suffering and injustice. Rather, being oppressed and/or excluded can leave us more complex because of the disruption to the ways we see ourselves and the world. After all, hurt people hurt people. When hurt people dominate conversations about social justice, it is unrealistic to expect sure-footed and perfect discussions that are about the greater good rather than settling scores. We shouldn't allow anyone to go unchallenged when the conversation veers away from equality. To do so will only cause pain in the long run. The reason why we are where we are is because power went unchecked and unopposed for a very long time; too many people looked the other way for the sake of convenience. We must not let the same thing happen again under different circumstances. To do so will lead to yet another imbalance that we will have to rectify.

Comprehending the paradox of power

We should want to learn from the past. We need to examine what has not worked and resulted in change and why. We can see where we are: we all start from a position in which some have more power than others, but we *all* have *some*. How can we reach a consensus on how to redistribute it in a fairer way for us all? What is the best way to resist the urge to control and dominate others? We know more than ever about how we think – what makes us tick – how can we use this knowledge to change? It is one thing to observe that others have to change (we do that very well), but how do we fully comprehend that this work has to be done in each and every one of us? How do we truly understand that we can do more together only if we constrain our need to control and dominate? What would happen if every person were committed to this self-examination and self-control?

We dominate to feel safe; we take from others to keep what's ours. But a paradoxical truth about power is that we have to keep it and give it away simultaneously. If we were to understand it in this way, we would become more comfortable about sharing it. A new level of trust could be built, with honesty at the foundation, and we would have to tell the ugly truth about power: we like it in the places where we want it; we give it away only when, for some reason, it's easier not to have it. There are times when, in our insecurity and inability to have power over ourselves, we try to coerce others. What if, instead, we were continually giving and receiving power? What if we didn't need all the power to change the status quo but, rather, just enough to work on the areas of injustice to which we felt called?

11

Does allyship work?

'A voice for the voiceless' is one of my least favourite phrases. It sums up much of the way in which modern allyship[1] works: that is, speaking for and over those we say we are supporting.

Why would someone want to be somebody else's voice? Most people like to speak for themselves and have the opportunity to tell their stories as they see fit. At its best, allyship facilitates bridging gaps to achieve results. At its worst, it involves privileged people making all the decisions about how to help, despite the fact that they themselves might feel patronized and overlooked if someone were to go from facilitating change to standing with them in a role that resembles ownership. We all have a voice: we either have to be encouraged to use it or others have to be encouraged to listen. While it might be acceptable to *amplify* someone's voice, it is not acceptable to *be* his or her voice; that is a level of control we should never seek.

In recent years, we have been educated about not finishing the sentences of someone who has a speech impediment. I have struggled to be patient in such circumstances because I think I know what the person is going to say, so I want to help. Unfortunately, by being impatient, I draw attention to the impediment and embarrass the person. I silence him or her, even though that wasn't my intention. The impact of speaking for others means that we silence them, maintaining the status quo and the idea that certain groups cannot advocate for themselves. This way of people associating themselves with a cause is so common, it is now the default setting for social-justice activism.

While there are appropriate times to speak up for others, we should also consider how we might encourage them to speak up for themselves. For example, we could let others speak for themselves while we back them up publicly and privately. Rescuing them all the time isn't actually helpful, even when they are grateful. It does not allow them to build the necessary resilience to advocate for themselves.

When a privileged person asks, 'Why do I, a White woman, have to speak up for people to take notice?' the answer is that, by the act of speaking, she is reaffirming the belief that only people in privileged positions – people with voices – will be heard. The groups being helped might come to believe this, too; the saviour dynamic is maintained. The 'voiceless' keep coming back for help and those with voices are continually helping – for ever.

Some groups of people certainly have more agency in certain situations than do others, but does their language promote change or does it maintain the unhealthy dynamic that they are trying to change? Often, if we investigate the chain of events that raises the profile of a cause, before allyship is in evidence, we see that the 'voiceless and powerless' have managed to make others hear them. Allyship has merely amplified those voices. Some nuance in how we approach allyship is required if we want to communicate successfully to find solutions. Rather than assuming allies should be the voice of a group struggling for equality, we should remind everyone of how that group has already voiced its experiences and consider how best to amplify that voice.

Boundaries

My parents have never been, and are still not, my friends, which is fine; I have friends. Some Jamaican parents can be this way. There are many sayings that help to keep this power dynamic in place:

'You must think mi and yuh is size.' ('You must think we are on the same level.')
'Big people talking.' ('This is an adult conversation.')
'I'm not one of yuh likkle friends.' ('Don't speak to me like that.')

I didn't have any say in how I was parented, although, as I mentioned earlier, I thought that I did. The relationship involved the establishing of a hierarchy in which the children were, of course, in the less dominant position. A similar dynamic operates in some contexts of allyship or association. Certain people are continually highlighting how they're 'helping' and continually talking about which privilege they have and how they are using it. This repetition keeps the status quo established and is very unhelpful. For the people who believe that they have no agency, and who are continually told that they don't have any and that the dynamic will never change, there is little hope of change.

In some cases, the children dominate the relationship rather than the parents. Usually, children are not as self-aware as adults; they tend to be single-minded about receiving the things they need because their survival depends on it. When they are babies, they require food and warmth, and their nappies have to be changed frequently. Then, as they grow, they discover that they need more things and find more ways to demand them. When children work out that there are few boundaries, and that they have your attention and some leverage, they incessantly demand instant gratification. This illustrates how extreme some relationships involving allyship can become.

Sometimes, in the discourse on gender, we can go from being pro women to anti men while requesting that men support us. Who wants to be associated with something that goes entirely against their interests? When equality is what we seek, then we must ask whether our stance is one with which the other side can and will ally itself. Allyship that is not founded on honesty can quickly become sour because a dishonest relationship can result in offence. The degree of offence is largely dictated by the person who is offended. Offence can occur when someone crosses an invisible, personal line. However, it's difficult to decide where a line is at a time when boundaries around acceptable behaviour and language are being redrawn.

Is there such a thing as a perfect ally? It's doubtful: human allies come with baggage, blind spots and biases, despite wanting to do the right thing. Those who have suffered injustice also have baggage, blind spots and biases. We would all benefit from remembering this when we interact.

In some cases, the saviour-and-victim dynamic might alter, especially as power and privilege shift. Allies who have fought beside us might be surprised and sad when liberation comes because we no longer need them. But fighting for liberation is not just a project; it's about winning access to a more just society for all. When we look at history, it might be fair to say that civil rights movements wouldn't have been effective without allies. However, Black people were already fighting for themselves before allies joined the cause and continued to do so afterwards.

No one will ever be as passionate about our own liberation as we are. In general, we fight hard for something that we believe in, particularly when our backs are against the wall. We should be encouraged to continue the fight rather than to outsource it to a privileged ally. That is what it means to have agency over ourselves and our circumstances. So, while allyship can provide support, it should not be allowed to take over the whole work. While it is valid that White people should dismantle racism because they built it, those most affected by it have a vested interest in sharing in the dismantling. Let's tear bigotry down together so that we can all be part of rebuilding society in a way that works for everyone.

Usually, people tend to build in the way that they have in the past, because it has always worked for them. To build something new requires collaboration, and collaboration works best when there is mutual respect. Relationships based on allyship are healthy only when we recognize who has which advantages or disadvantages, when there is respect for each other's agency, and when each of the allied parties recognizes the other's right to say yes or no. We must build relationships that allow honest communication because there usually has to be some sort of compromise. For us all to share this space together, we must say that we are all preferred so that no one is. We must recognize that we have different abilities, gifts, skills and talents for this important work of changing our communities for the better.

There will be a degree of discomfort while negotiating truly beneficial allyship. There will be times when we struggle against the tide with others and feel that we're on the verge of being swept away. When we are truly allied in the cause, though, there is a grace that comes with it when we are not, we cannot stand it because, deep down, we don't believe what we're saying or doing. Speaking about the positive aspects of standing with others is essential precisely because bringing change is challenging work, much of which goes against the things we naturally crave; we crave acceptance from as many people as possible and, sometimes, standing up for what is right doesn't deliver it. No matter who we are, we desire recognition for our good deeds, to have power and to be looked up to and admired for fighting the good fight; it is alluring to be viewed in such a light. Although we never like to think that our contribution is a performance for which we want to be recognized, we must examine our motives for helping. Are we doing so to feel good or to be good?

We can't ignore the fact that some of the mistrust between communities is because some people promise things that they don't mean, so they don't follow through. It's why we're often not sure, until some time has passed, if those times of focus on certain social injustices are indeed moments of great change. It's only with hindsight that we see whether or not there have been any positive outcomes.

Not understanding the issues, the communities or the injustices faced can result in a misalignment between what society needs and what we do. There are examples of commercial brands that get something like this incredibly wrong very publicly. One such was Pepsi, which was accused of 'co-opting police brutality' and exhibiting gross insensitivity about social-justice issues in 2017.[2] Allyship can never be done without adequate representation from the community concerned, and no one person or way of thinking should represent that community because it won't be monolithic. And, although people might aim to be allies, they can't just decide to be. The people or communities they come alongside will indicate whether or not they truly are.

Is this a performance?

With regard to allyship, we can become frustrated with the lack of outcomes when we ask for performances while what we need is change. In some cases, a community says that others must and should speak up for it. There is no harm in one group speaking up for another when it's authentic, when they believe it and when they have found their own courage to stand up to their families, friends and colleagues. But their action will lack conviction if they're shamed into acting. They will probably do only what they were asked and no more.

If we are not mindful, allyship can become a one-way street, with a list of demands that provoke performance-based actions which meet the letter, but not the spirit, of the change we want to see. Anti-racist activism is a case in point. No one likes to be called a racist, and many people genuinely want racism to end. Nevertheless, the relationship between the people helping and those being helped can quickly become political and lose all the relational aspects that make an alliance work. Relationships can be damaged easily when the helpers and the helped see one another as a means to an end. Initial goodwill can be used up quickly when we want to help people as we see fit. It can also disappear when those of us who have faced injustice – and who are passionate about our cause being seen, heard and rectified – try to involve others with no direct link to the injustice. Here, we can stray into different territory, where help is demanded and expected, with no questions asked, no challenge made and an insistence on complete loyalty. There will be those who are willing to help in such a way, which might be described as uncomfortably comfortable. Everyone has limits regarding how they can be involved, and it cannot be only on the terms of the person requesting the help. Equally, those who want to help should not dictate the terms of their aid.

Allyship must be by mutual consent. Without consent and willingness on both sides, the old power structures are maintained: one party dominates and the other acquiesces. There is no compromise or agreement to disagree about some aspects. There has to be equity in allyship; accepting behaviour we don't agree with does not fit into this category. Shared values have to play a part. No communities are monolithic, so wherever we choose to lend our support, there will be people whose views align with ours. We should seek them out.

We must also be honest with ourselves about the level at which allies can become involved with causes that aren't theirs; all of us have issues and constraints. Now, this is not to challenge the existence of original injustice in any way: racism exists; misogyny exists; xenophobia exists. Like the wind, bigotry might be hard to see, but we can identify the effects it has in a variety of situations. Potential allies might choose not to challenge injustice because they might suffer loss of opportunity, personal or professional. In other cases, they might not believe that there is a problem but won't say so. Even so, we should not shame people into standing up for causes in which they don't believe, even when they themselves think they should. It would be better to see what they might choose to do if left alone. It does no good to manipulate others into becoming allies before they are ready to do so, only for them to be called virtue-signallers[3] when they can't follow through. A symptom of an unhealthy dynamic is the lack of freedom to express true thoughts and feelings. Disagreement should not dismiss other people's experiences; we all come to the fight against injustice from different perspectives.

The moment of need

Support is understood differently by different people. It might sound complex but, in fact, it's what we should aspire to – to treat people as individuals and to help in the most relevant way.

Human beings naturally categorize other human beings, but it can be dehumanizing. The term 'refugees' stops us acknowledging separate individuals; instead, we think of a faceless sea of people. Nevertheless, refugees are humans who experience the full range of emotions, as we do. In their own countries, they might have been better off and more highly qualified than we are, but we identify them as weak and powerless victims who need our help, which can make us feel strong and powerful. Similarly, we might look down on those who use food banks. We don't see the parents or grandparents who have dignity, hopes and dreams, and who like a little luxury, or the children who like sweet treats. Rather, we see incapable people who should be grateful for anything they're given. When I buy food for the food bank, I only buy products I would eat. Recently, there was a complaint on social media about people buying crisps and chocolate biscuits for food banks. Just because someone is in need doesn't mean that they should be denied a small luxury. It may not be essential to life but it can provide a little bit of joy.

Sometimes, we think that the people we help don't deserve any more than scraps of goodness. Imagine that you'd left your purse or wallet at home and you asked a colleague to lend you some cash for lunch. How would you feel if he or she were to reply, 'Sure, but you can have only a basic lunch because I'm helping you', particularly if that colleague then bought something rather more upmarket for himself or herself? You would probably be grateful, because you needed to eat lunch, but slightly resentful at the way the help was given. How much worse would you feel if your colleague were to capture the moment of 'generosity' for a social-media post? We must – when we say we want to help people – watch out for the pity, and the patronizing and pandering attitudes that often creep in.

'Stop centring yourself' is a phrase that comes up repeatedly in the allyship space. Most of us spend a lot of time thinking about ourselves and how we appear to others, which takes plenty of concentration most of the time. When interacting with others, particularly when we attempt to listen to them sympathetically, we try to find common ground with them and let them know that we are kind and good and care about them. So we might stop listening and talk about similar things we've experienced, or offer solutions, when it is neither appropriate nor helpful, and might actually be quite narcissistic.

What we do with our internal thought-processes matters. When it comes to discussing issues around disadvantage and people who lack agency, how do we really see ourselves in relation to them? When we say to someone, 'We are going to use our privilege to help you', how would that sound if it were said to us? Would we feel patronized? We should let the other person identify what our privilege means for him or her; the power isn't always where we think it is in these scenarios.

Sometimes, when we can't help ourselves, being helped makes us resentful of those providing the aid. The knowledge that we don't have the tools to help ourselves hurts our pride. However, we should acknowledge when our needs can be met only through others using their advantage and agency. We all need help at some point in life. Ultimately, we should help as we would like to be helped; we should ask for help as we would like to be asked.

When we feel entitled to receive help we might stop seeing someone's humanity and view them as nothing more than a resource. I was once fascinated by a friend's baby who couldn't walk, but who wanted to get to the other side of the room. This baby worked out that, by raising his arms to a line of people, who would pick him up and put him down in succession, he could get to the other side. Humans are programmed to get what they want as conveniently as possible. It's not that they're purposely trying to use others; they are simply thinking of themselves, their needs and their desires.

Communication must change

Allyship in its most positive form is an understanding rooted in a relationship between individuals and/or communities. It involves understanding an issue not only socially but also mentally and emotionally. It is the alternative to confrontation; it can result in hearts and minds being changed. The aim of allyship should always be long-lasting change and, when it is, the ways we stand with others, the conversations we have and the actions we take are different.

Passionate, dynamic and unrepentant activists often start a conversation that more pragmatic people wouldn't begin; they raise the profile of a cause. Although swift, public and raw reactions have their place, it is hard for that style of communication to embed lasting change. At some point, however, people and communities on both sides of an injustice have to learn to understand each other, which is where relational allyship has its place. An ally can be part of the solution, a bridge of sorts, before moving aside. Rarely does one person or group solve big issues or even turn the dial of progress for everyone. It is misguided to think so. Nevertheless, we can all turn the dial – the point of standing with others is to be the agents of change together. We can all be a part of a great shift, especially if we were to consider what we might do regarding types of injustice other than those with which we're directly concerned. How would we participate?

On both sides of allyship, we all have the capability to misuse and mistreat one another, which makes it problematic when we become involved as a result of having the wrong motives. To pretend that we never have self-serving or misguided intentions is probably a sign that we don't understand ourselves, never mind other people. If we don't acknowledge the gaps between what we think we're doing, what other people think we're doing and what's actually happening, further damage might be caused.

When we remove unrealistic expectations of what it is to be great allies and the need to tell others how to be great allies, we will progress into a more mutually beneficial place. We will see those engaging in allyship simply as decent human beings standing against injustice.

12

Privilege, power and allyship

When we think about achieving positive, enduring change, we must also consider how privilege, power and allyship can work together in harmony. Once we have a clearer understanding of how these three operate in our lives, then we are better able to understand our part in making a difference.

As we have seen, it is possible for us to have more or less privilege than we think. We also have to look at advantage in tandem with agency. For example, someone might have White, male privilege, but he may not have a lot of power in a given situation. His ability to help others will be limited; while he might not be able to be an ally in terms of influencing others, he could offer emotional support.

If we want to stand with people in a way that counts, we must be honest about whether we can help or we are hindering those we want to support. We sometimes look for support from people who seem to have the right power but who may not have the privilege to go with it, so we might need to think carefully about how they could help. We should also consider if the conditions are right – whether we have enough power and privilege – to advocate for ourselves. More often than not, we do have the agency and the advantage to speak for ourselves. We should also assess when others have enough of the right tools to help themselves, and if our support is just an added bonus. Even so, we shouldn't be shy of stepping in and acting when those we want to help aren't able to help themselves, particularly if we are passionate about change. Conversely, when we need help, we must not be afraid to ask for it. We should all set aside both pride and hesitancy, and do whatever it takes to achieve the goal of a just world and equity for all.

Impact

With regard to interactions, when we personally have less at stake, we can stand with others in a way that is likely to have a greater impact and which is less likely to cause tension than when we have a lot to lose.

I remember experiencing an injustice that had little impact on me beyond irritation. However, I knew that many others would be affected by a power dynamic that was at play. It got under my skin, so I wrote a letter of complaint. I knew the other people couldn't or wouldn't complain because of possible ramifications for them so, due to the sensitivity of the situation, I warned them before I wrote the letter. Because there was nothing I needed or wanted from those I wrote to, I wasn't worried about the consequences and was happy to sign my name at the bottom of the letter. At no point, however, did I believe that I was the only person who could solve the problem. Rather, I understood that I could play a part in moving the conversation along, and it cost me little or nothing to do so. There are those who might say that the lack of cost meant I wasn't exhibiting true allyship. I would disagree; pain doesn't always have to be part of finding solutions. Sometimes, however, the fight for justice will require pain and sacrifice; we shouldn't always expect to be comfortable.

When we look at some of the serious injustices in society and wonder what it will take to rectify them, we have to consider that we are part of the answer. It may be that, no matter how well we communicate something to make an impact, our efforts don't pan out – but we must try. The goal of communication should not simply be to make people feel uncomfortable. To do so is not always an effective tactic for creating change. *But*, sometimes, people will feel uncomfortable when confronted with injustice for which they are responsible. Unfortunately, there are those who change only when shamed, but that position should never be the point from which we start.

In seeking the sweet spot for triggering change, we should be alert for the moments when our power and privilege are aligned. For example, it may be that those who try to help us can't, although the intention might be appreciated. However, it's also frustrating when those without any power believe they can step in and act on our behalf. It betrays a stereotypical view and a certain arrogance because they have failed to take the time to understand the issues and how they affect both them and us. For my part, when I approach a conversation, I am aware that I have little power but some privilege (such as access to certain contacts), which indicates the part I can play in finding a solution.

We must remain aware of the gap between what we believe to be happening and what is happening. What people tell us about privilege and how we actually experience life are not the same, and, deep down, many of us know that all is not as it seems. We must remember that the relationship between power and privilege is complicated. There are times when people can do nothing to help; it is valid to recognize this truth.

Relationship

Advantage, agency and association: these three factors work well only when rooted in relationship. We often don't think profoundly about how we speak to others concerning injustice. We speak, write and share without committing to communicating in a powerful way. Provided we communicate to be understood, rather than just to vent, we can begin to bring about change. The first obstacle to overcome is deciding how to have necessary conversations in the first place, with whom and when.

Times of crisis are when we start to think about those things that desperately need change. While a time of crisis might be the best time for action, it is not the best one for having nuanced conversations. Emotions run high and the urge to do something is strong. Groups are polarized, and people make remarks to draw attention; in the process, they get things wrong and cause offence. Feelings can either get in the way, causing us to lose momentum at a moment we have it, or they can provide the potential to push for change in a meaningful way. How we communicate in such moments is crucial. There is no doubt that people dig their heels in when emotions are running high, unless they are truly open to change. It would be wise, therefore, to consider how to grapple with issues when 'nothing is happening'. By having the conversations when the emotions of those involved are calmer and participants are thinking clearly about how they might contribute, there will be greater progress. Then, when the significant moments arise, everyone involved in the conversation will have moved on from their entrenched positions.

Who decides what's appropriate?

The nature of life means that we often go through the motions. We don't always notice the dynamics that are maintaining the status quo. By exploring how agency, advantage and association work well together, we can gauge how effective we might be in tackling injustice. Of course, we have to decide together how to use them well.

When we have agency over others, how can we seek to understand and listen? What do we fail to notice in a conversation? To whom are we accountable and from whom do we take advice? When we do not build genuine connections over time with those to whom we want to lend our power, it will be far too tricky to join them in the heat of battle. In the rush to be seen as the good guys, who are doing the right thing, we might fail to consider whether we are harming as much as we are helping or, indeed, if we are helping at all. We have to be careful; using our power can be damaging.

Association must be by mutual consent. When one party dominates another, the relationship is unbalanced. Sometimes, the power and privilege involved are not what one side thinks they are; neither is the relationship. Some allies have the advantage of having friends in the group, of sharing similarities or characteristic intersections or of being thought of as associates. However, when there is an imbalance of power, it usually arises because a group considers its potential allies patronizing, does not trust their motives and believes that they maintain the systemic gap.

When considering how best to integrate agency, advantage and association, we must review our relationships. We must be courageous enough to ask the other parties how they experience the relationship. Do they think we have more privilege than they do? Are we telling people, without knowing the full facts or their history, that we will use our advantage and agency to help them? Are we emphasizing the gap? We should also certainly be asking questions such as 'How can we help? What would be helpful to you? Where are you already gaining ground? Where can we collaborate?' We shouldn't assume that we are the ones who can save people who might not need saving – at least, not in the way we choose to dictate. After all, we can really only ever see the view from where we sit.

The third way

Wouldn't it be great if we could actually see the view from where someone else sits? Unfortunately, we can't, even when we want to; rather, we usually try to interpret the view we can't see. So our assumptions about others' thoughts and situations will always be unbalanced or distorted, which is why we must be particularly careful when choosing to play devil's advocate. First, we should be careful because evil doesn't need an advocate. Second, because, by doing so, we introduce a third perspective to the conversation, which may be unhelpful. For instance, when someone asks for help or advice, or tries to tell us about an injustice, rather than listen properly, we intervene and say, 'Just playing devil's advocate here. What if so-and-so didn't mean that? What if they are not [*insert appropriate word or phrase*]? Perhaps it's not what you think it is.' The problem is, of course, that we weren't present at the time of the incident, so we can't – and don't – know what happened. Even though we might choose to play devil's advocate because we like the person accused of the injustice, we can't entirely speak for that person. Doing so complicates the discussion, which probably won't help to calm the situation. By playing devil's advocate, we make the mistake of thinking that we know how others are thinking, which, of course, is neither correct nor possible.

We must resist the temptation to fill in the blanks. We have to give others time and space, and listen attentively to their stories, even when we don't believe what we hear. After all, we all have those gaps between what we believe and what is true. We must be gracious to others and accept that others' situations can be rather more complex than they might at first appear.

The times when someone offering a third perspective is welcome is when the person offering it has witnessed and been observant and has thought about the discourse from the start. Certain people are very wise and experienced, and can offer advice, provide warnings and make helpful observations to both sides about what they've heard or read. Nevertheless, we have to understand that people are free to refuse an additional perspective, have the right to choose their own paths and make their own mistakes.

It takes all kinds

Those of us who have power and privilege often think that we know what is best for others. Sometimes we do, but we must accept that using our agency to force through something others want does not necessarily help.

When emotions run high during a conversation, I tend to refrain from saying that I don't agree with the other person's approach, unless we have a good relationship or I'm asked for my opinion. I don't hold my peace because I'm happy to see other people fail. After all, who am I to say that the approach will not work, just because I might choose another way? Also, different people can get away with doing and saying different things. Those things that I am not comfortable doing or saying might work for others; paths to power are forged through trial and error.

It takes different kinds of people to crack the justice conversation open. Some people are naturally antagonistic; some are conciliatory; and yet others are persuasive or influential. There are even those who kick off a conversation by making outrageous comments. We need all these different styles of advocacy to bring about change. In different spaces, people will behave in different ways. Those who have established relationships in a space, and so will remain there, might feel constrained and will watch what they say. But when we are strangers, we might have more power if those in the space are inclined to hear the opinions of outsiders. What we wouldn't have is the privilege of relationship, so we wouldn't know whom we might be offending – which can work well. We would have little investment in the existing relationships, so we could be rather more forthright in what we say because we could leave without looking back. If strangers do offend, conciliatory souls might use their particular agency to try to smooth ruffled feathers by offering different ways to look at the comments, thereby taking the sting out of any offence.

The invitation to serve and do our best to be part of a specific conversation is to understand what our power and privilege are, then we can identify how to stand up for a cause. Understanding is key: when we discover that we aren't changing minds, we have to examine how we might be hindering, rather than facilitating, progress towards our goal.

When it comes to self-examination, the biggest obstacle is the ego. It hinders much progress. A lot of the time, people discussing social-justice issues talk just for effect rather than to effect change. Others use their privilege purely to further their own personal agendas or, worse, fill their pockets. In these cases, their 'contributions' to the cause are not helpful; they don't move anything along. In fact, more than anything, they tend to antagonize others. So how do we guard against this? Well, it's not enough for those types of people to get out of their own way or anyone else's. Again, self-examination and understanding are key.

If we have a talent for throwing word-bombs into a conversation that clear paths for those coming behind, we must resist the temptation just to create shock and awe. If we don't, we will seek to say wilder and wilder things, and our reputation for being outrageous (if effective) will overshadow, or possibly take over from, the cause. Also, because justice must always be our Pole Star, our presence in the discourse might become problematic. It can seem as if word-bombers deliberately want to cause as many people as possible to feel uncomfortable, taking pleasure in their discomfort. Of course, if other people sense that this is the aim, it undermines trust, which shouldn't be anyone's goal in social-justice discourse. After all, what does that do for eventual unity?

For those of us who seek to be conciliatory, we must be careful not to dismiss some people's experiences to make others feel better; we must be prepared to sit in discomfort during the awkward silence that can follow a difficult exchange. We must resist the temptation to mend fences immediately. Some things take time, requiring an organic healing process and rebuilding of trust. There are times when we try so hard to overcome an offence that we want to forget what has happened and move on, but we should do so only once we have learnt the lessons. Criticism is never pleasant but we must not hide from it.

Conversations around justice can stall when we try to control other people. We think that everyone must completely agree with us for progress to be made. We advocate difference and then shut down other ways of approaching a conversation. On occasion, I've noted my profound discomfort with people who use (what I consider to be) crude language when addressing others. I feel particularly uncomfortable when the target of the words may not be at fault, which is how I also feel when complaining in a restaurant: the person I complain to might not be the one at fault, but he or she is an employee of the restaurant – part of its structure – which is why he or she is receiving the complaint. When I do complain, I'm careful how I do so. There are times when I've doubted that others have thought through *how* they complain or considered those to whom they complain. Nevertheless, I have to remember that this discomfort is personal. My feelings can't dictate what other people do.

In some circumstances, we might be able to use our power or privilege to shut an exchange down because we believe that there is a better way. However, the people involved might not need our advocacy. They might have considered different factors and are seeking other outcomes. We must assume that we all have different agendas, rather than thinking that shared characteristics mean shared visions. We must improve our communication to clarify on which points we converge and on which we diverge. Related to this is the temptation to rail against the mainstream spaces where we don't feel welcomed. If we do rant about them, we can, in our turn, alienate others, who might not agree with us on every point and yet want to fight alongside us for justice. We can forget that at the core of much of what we're fighting for is the universal desire to belong.

Power and privilege are factors that we all have and can use; those of us who believe ourselves to be on the wrong side of justice must examine how we use ours. Pretending that we don't have power and privilege is the quick route out of personal responsibility and into the misuse of them – we think that because our words and actions don't affect others, we can do and say what we please. If that were true, why speak at all? Why act? It's precisely because we know we will have an impact that we speak, and we must take responsibility for doing so. What we do counts in a space where we have privilege or influence. When we all acknowledge that our power (whatever form it takes) does have an impact, progress will be quicker.

To examine how we use power and privilege, we should ask ourselves the following: are we accelerating change? Are we empowering people to be more than their circumstances or are we validating hopelessness? Are we championing the dichotomy of 'them and us', rather than a unified 'we'? Do we really believe that there can and will be change? We must be especially mindful of these questions when dealing with young people who are still hopeful that things can change; we must be careful not to repackage our own fatigue as wisdom.

There is a difference between raising awareness and killing hope. We so often think that, because we can't do something, it can't be done. We usually find it hard to accept that someone else achieves what we have merely attempted. Unlike the successful campaigner, we might not have had the power and privilege or the luxury of advocates to help us make progress. This envy exposes the gap between who we want to be and who we are; it makes us feel a little insecure. Envy and insecurity must be pushed aside for the sake of ultimate victory. We must focus on the vision. If we were to do so, it would reveal whether or not the story we show the world and who we truly are align.

Pathways versus conduits

For advocacy to work, advocates must use their privilege to create more pathways for access to power for others. They can do so by making introductions, stepping back and letting new relationships form. It is not necessary for advocates to remain as go-betweens or continual conduits to power once they've opened the way for those they support.

When this occurs, we know that we are truly using power, privilege and allyship in harmony to bring about change. Without helping people to build their own bridges, power structures and paths for success, we are simply maintaining the same structures that have always existed. When we explore how we are privileged and where we have power, we can identify the spaces in which we can effect change. Often our privilege will make us feel that we have the right to demand gratitude or continual involvement with people and their cause because we have helped them in some small way. It would be great if they were to continue to include us, but we should be willing to step aside; we shouldn't expect them to be indebted to us for ever. So we must be self-aware and secure enough to know how and when to limit our involvement. This self-examination is the work.

Privilege, power and allyship work best when we do not centre ourselves in the issue concerned. Our story and view of ourselves means that we usually want other people to see who we are, which is why some people are more offended at being called unjust than they are by acknowledging their own part in injustice. By giving priority to our need to be seen as good and right – rather than to finding the best way to reach solutions – we are holding progress back. We must all assess when we are in a position to advise, take action or advocate, and when, instead, all we have to do is facilitate a conversation and then step back.

Unhelpful advocacy sees the one being helped as lesser than the advocate, and incapable of making wise decisions or taking action the 'right' way. So the advocate micro-manages and is like a parent overseeing a child. Obviously, if the advocate were to have the skills that are needed, then how they would be shared or used could only ever be decided by mutual consent. We must accept that our way isn't necessarily the 'right' way, just because it is mainstream or generally accepted. We must also accept that we might be helping someone who has knowledge and skills but little access to opportunity.

Understanding the complexities of effective advocacy is key. We must examine our own motives honestly and explore how we might be hindering rather than helping. When we try to support people we believe to be our inferiors, it is hard to acknowledge that we don't think of them as equal, but we achieve nothing by denying our fallible, human thoughts. Most of us have been conditioned to think a certain way, and it is that which we must identify and rectify. We must continually explore our thoughts and realign them, which will allow better outcomes for us all.

13

Better conversations

We all believe in justice. But we are going to have to work to push our natural reactions aside so that we can communicate effectively to find solutions. A look at broadcast news, social media and newspapers reveals that our current methods for trying to solve social and justice issues cause hurt and pain. Sympathy, good intentions and meaning well aren't enough in the face of exploitative, unkind and disrespectful behaviour towards people who are different. It's easy to see such unpleasant behaviour in others, but we also have to examine ourselves to identify whether we are conduits for or barriers to justice.

The journey towards a better society starts with honesty regarding ourselves. It's easy to think that the problems are external, but we can and must seek out the propensity for injustice that lurks inside us and work towards eradicating it. This process is not about beating ourselves up or becoming stuck in a cycle of virtuous guilt; it's about admitting that we each have to make changes. We have to consider how our prejudices are preventing us from acting justly and fairly. We have to explore fearlessly those occasions when we have not been the human beings we want to believe we are. We have to choose to close the gap between who we want to be and who we truly are. Without honesty concerning ourselves we can never truly be honest with others. We cannot address our biases when we refuse to admit that we have them. Some of our biases are ugly; some of the language we have used about other people has been ugly; denying the humanity of others and reducing them to stereotypes are ugly; and preventing access to opportunities for minorities is ugly. Rather than indulging in shame when we recognize our biases, we should choose to move on and up, holding ourselves to a higher standard of behaviour that promotes equality.

Let us choose to be honest about our shortcomings and how we lack knowledge, seeing them as an opportunity to change. Let us be honest about:

- the times when it has been a chore to include and think of others, and so we failed to do so;
- how we felt about and treated others who had something that we didn't think they deserved;
- how we dismissed those we didn't know because of the prejudiced things we'd heard;
- how we find it easier to dismiss others on sight than to treat them like the individuals they are.

Let's be honest and think about how we begin to move past all that.

Without admitting that we have blind spots, we will not choose to broaden our horizons. Honesty will allow us to see how we need to change to be better equipped to fight for a fairer world. This is challenging and necessary. When we have chosen to be honest, we must remember that we are human and everyone has biases but once we are aware of our own, we can work to compensate for them. Doing so will help us not to commit the mistakes that have previously prevented us from working towards better outcomes.

Language in the arena of social justice has been divisive. We usually begin our discourses from places of misunderstanding and entrenched thinking. We use similar words but ascribe to them different meanings. Honesty about language can lessen tension in the conversation and make it more productive. What if we were to begin by asking, 'What do you mean by "woke", "cancel culture" and "racism"? This is what I think of when I hear those words'? We could also start the conversation by highlighting that we don't want to offend others and by saying what offends us. At times, we will understand how the terms are being used but we still won't agree; indeed, we might be genuinely exasperated. That, though, is no reason to adopt a patronizing or antagonistic tone, which will only undermine our efforts to influence, persuade or convince others. Rather, we should aim to keep the discourse calm. After all, if we are antagonistic, who wins? What do we gain? Whose minds do we change?

For the sake of winning a point, we often walk away with nothing. If we behave in such a way, how truly committed can we be to change?

We often enter a conversation 'knowing' that those on the other side of it are wrong; so our ears and hearts are closed. If we are not prepared to listen to other points of view, perhaps it's best not to enter into social-justice discourses. We can never help someone to understand what we mean and believe if we don't listen to what they mean and believe. As we listen, we often discover that we have more in common with one another, especially on the 'what' and the 'why', although the 'how' is often a sticking point. Let's listen to what people say and what's behind what they say; we are all complex, come from a variety of backgrounds and have had different experiences.

Another useful question to ask during a conversation is, 'Why do you think that?' Some people's opinions don't necessarily spring from where we think they do. Without building a relationship with others, there's no way of knowing why they have arrived at certain opinions. The good thing about finding out more is that gaps in our knowledge can be filled. But those gaps can only be filled when we have acknowledged they are there – that we have blind spots.

Just listening to another's opinion isn't necessarily the same as *hearing* him or her. The statements people make may be only the tip of the iceberg, with the full intent and meaning left unsaid. We should try to listen with open hearts, especially about things we don't understand. I tend to ask friends to explain why they agree with something that makes no sense to me. Although their answers might not persuade me, I understand a little more about their reasons for believing as they do. I also try to be patient with people who take the time to listen carefully, although, when presented with new information, they don't change their opinions. In tandem with listening carefully, we should resist the temptation to rush to an answer. It's fine to admit that we need time let new questions and information sink in. With regard to the huge, often deeply personal issues of justice, listening has to look a bit different, and we must allow time for people to formulate genuine responses. And we can do all that while insisting that there must be change.

It is a huge challenge for us when others see things very differently; so, even when we acknowledge our common goals, how can we create space for change? Do we require people to share our opinions? Are we trying to sell our own visions? We are not and cannot be the thought police. We cannot make people behave or think justly. We can, however, create spaces in which we can listen carefully to them and accept that only one conversation will not bring about enduring change. Listening well and patiently will allow us to acquire an accurate frame of reference with which to begin to influence others.

When it comes to learning about various perspectives, we should accept that different people are at different stages: one person might be on step 97 while someone else is on step 11. We don't have to move at the same speed, but we do have to move forwards. Also, influencing and persuading others to understand an alternative point of view is rather more effective than forcing them to do so. We have to accept that other people are where they are in a conversation. To try to make them start where they are not means basing the discourse on a shaky foundation. Some people might think that this approach is nothing better than pandering to the other side, but when we go into a discussion convinced of our rightness, there is no space for disagreement and no space to manoeuvre. Arguments are rarely won; debates rarely change minds. Conversation, however, creates the space for minds to change. Nevertheless, creating space for meaningful discourse uses up emotional energy, so we should focus on what will bring about meaningful change.

Systemic structures and practices that maintain injustices and hold people back are all around. Systemic injustice is the toughest to call out and act against; it is so ingrained in society that many of us shrug our shoulders and mutter, 'It's just the way things are.' Taking on systemic injustice is not similar to talking to a racist family member or friend. While those interactions have an emotional and relational toll, fighting systemic issues requires persistence, patience, righteous anger and a willingness to make sacrifices. Institutions – such as the government, the police, the Church, the health-care system, the legal system and the media – that run and support society are not going to be changed by one conversation, one letter or one protest. However, sustained conversations, protest and action over a period of time might. When addressing institutional injustice, we have to use all our honesty and collaborate with others to produce change from the inside out.

There are many people who choose not to take on this kind of injustice because a quick victory is far from assured and there is little in the way of a feelgood factor during the process. Nevertheless, it is in the public arena that change is most desperately needed. Witnessing injustices must move us to action; we must never stop trying to make society fairer. We have to communicate with these institutions – many of which we fund – that we want change and we won't stop calling out injustice until we see change. We should never be quiet, allowing injustice to remain; we must loudly come against it. We should ensure that all groups know their rights and are able to communicate them when required. Entire communities should hold perpetrators to account when their rights are infringed, using the law when necessary.

When we witness unfairness, do we speak up if we have agency or influence? Are we willing to stand with those who are being unfairly treated, publicly if need be? Unjust systemic practices continue because people choose to assimilate rather than stop the cycle of abuse. We should collectively write open letters to our politicians, emphasizing that they would risk losing our votes were they not to take our concerns seriously. Those of us in lobby groups, pressure groups and think tanks could apply pressure to government by using data that reveal whether or not there has been progress and, if so, what progress has been made.

Negative stereotyping and categorizations of others dehumanize, but we communicate justice when we treat each person we encounter as an individual. We know how to treat those who resemble us well; so, deep down, we must also know when we fail to extend the same kindness and opportunity to everyone. When we feel uncomfortable with people we don't know, we must examine our thinking and biases. Why do we make assumptions about those who are unfamiliar? We should give others a chance by choosing to try to understand who they are and what they believe. Let's adjust our own lenses so that we can encompass other perspectives to gain accurate information about others. They might be horrible people but at least we have established that fact for ourselves. Other individuals are complex and we must allow for that; we are complex and we must allow for that too. We can extend this simple act of grace to everyone.

We should aim to enter interactions with others as we would like others to enter interactions with us. When we are behind a screen on social media, we can be emboldened to say things or to communicate in a style that can be regrettable. IF those we are communicating with or about were in front of us, what would we change? Free speech, while a right, comes with personal responsibility. No one gets everything right all the time. Our instincts can be strong, especially when we are upset or feel deeply about something, but they can also be wrong. We determine how we interact with others, so we must take responsibility for that too.

An unexpressed choice is still a choice. No one denies the need for an equal society; yet we have not managed to achieve an equal or equitable one. Many of those who run workplaces and places of worship say that they want their organizations to be inclusive but, despite many meetings and reams of reports, nothing changes. Behind each decision to change – or not – are people. While it may not be expressed, people have decided that they are not going to expand the culture around them to be fairer and more inclusive. They have simply, quietly chosen not to do the right thing. Currently, our culture requires assimilation but we must seek its expansion. We must consider a new way of being in which there is freedom and diversity of thought. Perhaps we have to change; perhaps not, but we mustn't close down the conversation too quickly.

How many times have we assumed that people have been recruited to our workplaces because they tick diversity boxes? By making such an assumption, we immediately devalue their contribution, particularly if we haven't taken into account their qualifications, skills and experience. How many times have we silenced their input as a result? Why do we feel the need to surround ourselves with people who resemble us in the workplace? Why would we want to force people who are different to leave, resulting in the loss of professional and cultural enrichment?

Those who may not be similar to us are still human beings with individual personalities and needs. We have to drop the walls so that we can all benefit from an exchange of different ideas and perspectives. Whatever our workplace (or other) culture, it is unlikely to be diminished by welcoming others. Coming to a new collaborative way of being isn't without friction, but there is no need to erase difference; we should celebrate it. It adds to our knowledge of the world, and to who and what we can all be together. When we respect and honour others, we can safely welcome new ideas and ways of being.

We are usually very sensitive concerning the things we care about. We care less about the things that aren't close to our hearts: this is the human way. But this attitude causes a great deal of offence. During our conversations, we have to accept that, at times, people will cause offence or be offended. Despite our best efforts, others might not take things well. Also, no matter how careful we are, some people are just waiting to be offended. Nevertheless, we must try hard not to offend. So it is best to be clear; clarity is kind. Therefore:

- we should not agree with things we don't agree with;
- we should not say things that we don't mean;
- we should not promise things that we can't deliver.

Doing any of these things breaks trust, which is vital when we are allied with others to fight against injustice.

Half-truths, not fully explained, are some of the greatest blocks to progress. When people believe themselves to have been misled, it results in hurt and betrayal. So we have to remember that we don't know what we don't know. We should be open about not having all the answers but be committed to finding them. Honesty and clarity are essential for the continued hope that change will come. Some of us have to accept the answers that we receive. We will not always like them but compromise might be necessary on the road to a shared, equitable future.

When we accept ourselves, we accept other people. Without this understanding, little change can happen. We must acknowledge that those attitudes we refuse to change are points of insecurity; they drive us into spaces where we look for validation that we are who we want to be. But no amount of external validation can reassure an insecure person. Truly secure people do the internal work of reconciling themselves with who and what they are – warts and all. Recognizing our own humanity allows us to be gracious towards others. Rigorous self-examination has to be as much a lifetime's work as anything else. After all, with whom do we spend the most time, if not ourselves? When we have pride in ourselves, we can begin to end the distinction between 'superior' and 'inferior', and expand our world to include other cultures.

We can be our best with and most accepting of others when we accept ourselves. By learning how to communicate with ourselves with care, we can communicate with others with care. It is only then that we can begin to communicate successfully with other beautiful, complex, messy individuals to build a better, fairer, more equal and equitable world.

Notes

Preface

1 Martin Luther King, Jr, 'Advice for living', in Clayborne Carson (ed.), *The Papers of Martin Luther King, Jr., Volume IV: Symbol of the movement, January 1957–December 1958* (Berkeley and Los Angeles, CA: University of California Press, 2000), 1–31 May 1958; see The Martin Luther King, Jr. Research and Education Institute, Stanford University <https://kinginstitute.stanford.edu/king-papers/documents/advice-linving-10>, accessed 10 June 2021.

1 Communicate for solutions

1 Dale Carnegie, *How to Win Friends and Influence People* (London: Vermilion, 1998), p. 124.

2 From 'The other America', a speech given at Stanford University in 1967; see The Martin Luther King, Jr. Center, 'In the final analysis' [Twitter post/video], 28 May 2020, <https://twitter.com/TheKingCenter/status/1266008254984982529?ref_src=twsrc%5Etfw%7Ctwcamp%5Etweetembed%7Ctwterm%5E1266008254984982529%7Ctwgr%5E%7Ctwcon%5Es1_&ref_url=https%3A%2F%2Ftheweek.com%2Fspeedreads%2F917022%2Friot-language-unheard-martin-luther-king-jr-explained-53-years-ago>, accessed 10 June 2021.

3 By 'narrative', I mean a story that has been shaped to reflect a certain perspective; it is not wholly objective.

4 Richard Rohr, *Eager to Love: The alternative way of Francis of Assisi* (London: Hodder & Stoughton, 2014), p. 94.

5 '[The] state or condition of being an ally: supportive association with another person or group . . . *specifically*: such association with the members of a marginalized or mistreated group to which one does not belong', see Merriam-Webster, 'Allyship', <www.merriam-webster.com/dictionary/allyship>, accessed 25 May 2021.

6 The *Concise Oxford English Dictionary* defines 'racism' as '1 the belief that each race or ethnic group possesses specific characteristics, abilities, or qualities that distinguish it as inferior or superior to another such group. 2 discrimination against or antagonism towards other races or ethnic groups based on such a belief'. 'Prejudice' is defined as a 'preconceived opinion that is not based on reason or actual experience' and as 'unjust behaviour formed on such a basis'.

7 '[To] treat or consider (a person or a group of people) as alien to oneself or one's group (as because of different racial, sexual, or cultural characteristics)', see Merriam-Webster, 'Other (verb)' <www.merriam-webster.com/dictionary/other>, accessed 31 May 2021.

8 For a brief overview of White privilege, see 'White privilege: What is it and how can it be used to help others?' BBC Newsround, 17 June 2020, <www.bbc.co.uk/newsround/52937905>, accessed 25 May 2020.

9 '[Aware] of and actively attentive to important facts and issues (especially issues of racial and social justice)', see Merriam-Webster, 'Woke', <www.merriam-webster.com/dictionary/woke>, accessed 31 May 2021.

2 Fake news

1 By 'singular narrative', I mean a belief that is narrow and biased. For example, beliefs such as 'all Black people are disadvantaged and are brought up by single mothers', 'all White people are racist' and 'working-class people who live on estates are violent' are singular narratives.

2 Claire Fallon, 'Where does the term "fake news" come from? The 1890s, apparently', *Huffington Post*, 24 March 2017, <www.huffingtonpost.co.uk/entry/where-does-the-term-fake-news-come-from_n_58d53c89e4b03692bea518ad?ri18n=true>, accessed 17 May 2021; see also Merriam-Webster, 'The real story of "fake news"' (n.d.), <www.merriam-webster.com/words-at-play/the-real-story-of-fake-news>, accessed 17 May 2021.

3 Lorraine Ali, 'Review: Sundance 2020: "Hillary" film takes on scandal allegations, bias and, yes, Bernie too', *Los Angeles Times*, 25 January

2020, <www.latimes.com/entertainment-arts/tv/story/2020-01-25/ review-sundance-2020-hillary-documentary-review>, accessed 17 May 2021.

4 Genelle Aldred, 'The extent to which language is weaponised is interesting' [Twitter post], 12.56 p.m., 13 June 2020, <https://twitter. com/genellealdred/status/1271773420229967873>, accessed 17 May 2021.

5 A report in the journal *Injury Prevention* revealed that in the 'countries for which comparable data were available, the annual average death rate from road injury was approximately 390 times that from international terrorism.' See N. Wilson and G. Thomson, 'Deaths from international terrorism compared with road crash deaths in OECD countries', *Injury Prevention*, vol. 11 (2005), pp. 332–3; a PDF of the article is available on the BMJ Journals website at <https:// injuryprevention.bmj.com/content/injuryprev/11/6/332.full.pdf >, accessed 10 June 2021.

6 Robin Yapp, 'Friends who last a lifetime', *Daily Mail* (n.d.), <www. dailymail.co.uk/femail/article-202987/Friends-lifetime.html>, accessed 10 June 2021.

7 Chimamanda Ngozi Adichie, *Half of a Yellow Sun* (London: 4th Estate, 2019).

8 Kayla Webley, 'How the Nixon–Kennedy debate changed the world', *Time*, 23 September 2010, <http://content.time.com/time/nation/ article/0,8599,2021078,00.html>, accessed 17 May 2020.

9 Ofcom, *Guidance Notes: Section six – Elections and referendums* (2017), pp. 4, 5 and 8, <www.ofcom.org.uk/__data/assets/pdf_ file/0034/99178/broadcast-code-guidance-section-6-march-2017.pdf>, accessed 17 May 2021.

4 A culture of confusion

1 Emotional intelligence helps us when we interact with others on a one-to-one basis. Cultural intelligence is a similar sort of wisdom applied more widely – to groups, communities and cultures.

2 Patrick Lencioni, *The Five Dysfunctions of a Team: A leadership fable* (San Francisco, CA: Jossey-Bass, 2002).

3 See Paul Lewis, 'Exploring the rise of populism: "It pops up in

unexpected places"', *The Guardian*, 22 June 2019, <www.theguardian.com/membership/2019/jun/22/populism-new-exploring-rise-paul-lewis>, and Brian Nolan, 'Why we can't just blame rising inequality for the growth of populism around the world', The Conversation (n.d.), <https://theconversation.com/why-we-cant-just-blame-rising-inequality-for-the-growth-of-populism-around-the-world-120951>; both accessed 10 June 2021.

4 For a definition of 'woke', see Ch. 1, note 9. See Ch. 1, note 8 for where to find an overview of White 'privilege'.

5 Charlotte Ruhl, 'Implicit or unconscious bias', Simply Psychology, 1 July 2020, <www.simplypsychology.org/implicit-bias.html>, accessed 10 June 2021.

6 See Ruhl, 'Implicit or unconscious bias'.

7 In April 2020, there were 5 female CEOs in the FTSE 100 out of 100 CEOs (data collected, 17 April 2020): see The Pipeline, Women Count 2020: Role, value, and number of female executives in the FTSE350, p. 2, <https://execpipeline.com/wp-content/uploads/2020/12/The-Pipeline-Women-Count-2020-1.pdf>, accessed 10 June 2021.

8 The Pipeline, Women Count 2020, p. 12.

9 YouGov, 'When in the UK, are you bothered when you hear those from a non-English speaking country talking to each other in their own language, or not?', 3 February 2020, <https://yougov.co.uk/topics/politics/survey-results/daily/2020/02/03/66818/3>, accessed 12 June 2021.

6 Blind spots

1 Quoted in Keosha Varela, 'Death row attorney Bryan Stevenson on 4 ways to fight against injustice' [blog], Aspen Institute, 20 July 2016, <www.aspeninstitute.org/blog-posts/death-row-attorney-bryan-stevenson-4-ways-fight-injustice>, accessed 19 May 2021.

2 For definitions of 'racism' and 'prejudice', see Ch. 1, note 6.

7 A singular narrative

1 A paraphrase of an online post by Carlos A. Rodríguez. See 'When we're not hungry for justice' [Facebook post], 9.44 a.m., 7 August 2019, <www.facebook.com/citizenshipandsocialjustice/posts/

when-were-not-hungry-for-justice-its-usually-because-were-too-full-with-privileg/2439141579479916>, accessed 22 May 2021.

2 '[The] practice or tendency of engaging in mass cancelling [withdrawal of support] as a way of expressing disapproval and exerting social pressure', see Merriam-Webster, 'Cancel culture', <www.merriam-webster.com/dictionary/cancel%20culture>, accessed 26 May 2021.

3 From an open letter written on 16 April 1963: see 'Letter from Birmingham Jail', Wikipedia (last modified 16 April 2021), <https://en.wikipedia.org/wiki/Letter_from_Birmingham_Jail>, accessed 11 June 2021.

4 See Kevin Arnscott, 'Winterval: The unpalatable making of a modern myth', *The Guardian*, 8 November 2011, <www.theguardian.com/commentisfree/2011/nov/08/winterval-modern-myth-christmas>, accessed 11 June 2021.

8 Saviours

1 For a definition of 'allyship', see Ch. 1, note 5.

9 A pack of privilege

1 See 'If someone doesn't understand privilege, show them this' [video], YouTube, uploaded 6 July 2018, <www.youtube.com/watch?v=ZZuucE4R65Q>, accessed 25 May 2021.

2 The origin of this proverb is unknown. However, a version of it originated in 1885 in Anne Isabella Thackeray Ritchie's novel, *Mrs Dymond*: 'If you give a man a fish, he is hungry in an hour. If you teach him to catch a fish, you do him a good turn.' More succinct versions, such as the one quoted here, have been attributed variously to the Navajo, Chinese and Italians.

3 Peggy McIntosh, 'White privilege: Unpacking the invisible knapsack', *Peace and Freedom Magazine*, July/August 1989, pp. 10–12; a PDF of the paper is available on the Alliance for Learning website, <http://allianceforlearning.co.uk/wp-content/uploads/2020/06/McIntosh-White_Privilege.pdf>, accessed 11 June 2021.

10 Power truths

1 '[The] capacity, condition, or state of acting or of exerting power', see Merriam-Webster, 'Agency', <www.merriam-webster.com/dictionary/agency>, accessed 26 May 2021.
2 For a definition of 'cancel culture', see Ch. 7, note 2.
3 Social-media platforms verify accounts to show that they are authentic. Verification can assign the qualities of credibility and trustworthiness to an account.

11 Does allyship work?

1 For a definition of 'allyship', see Ch. 1, note 5.
2 See Tom Batchelor and Christopher Hooton, 'Pepsi advert with Kendall Jenner pulled after huge backlash', *The Independent*, 5 April 2017, <www.independent.co.uk/arts-entertainment/tv/news/pepsi-advert-pulled-kendall-jenner-protest-video-cancelled-removed-a7668986.html>, accessed 11 June 2021.
3 Virtue signalling is 'the sharing of one's point of view on a social or political issue, often on social media, in order to garner praise or acknowledgment of one's righteousness from others who share that point of view, or to passively rebuke those who do not', see Dictionary.com, <www.dictionary.com/browse/virtue-signaling>, accessed 28 May 2021.